Collins
Irish
Grammar

HarperCollins Publishers
Westerhill Road
Bishopbriggs
Glasgow
G64 2QT
Great Britain

First Edition 2011

© HarperCollins Publishers 2011

Reprint 10 9 8 7 6 5 4 3 2 1 0

ISBN 978-0-00-739138-7

www.collinslanguage.com

A catalogue record for this book is
available from the British Library

Typeset by Davidson Publishing
Solutions, Glasgow

Printed in Great Britain by Clays Ltd,
St Ives plc

Acknowledgements
We would like to thank those authors
and publishers who kindly gave
permission for copyright material to be
used in the Collins Word Web. We would
also like to thank Times Newspapers Ltd
for providing valuable data.

SERIES EDITOR
Robert Scriven

MANAGING EDITOR
Gaëlle Amiot-Cadey

WRITTEN BY
Niall Comer

EDITOR
Teresa Alvarez

CONTRIBUTORS
Daphne Day
Val McNulty

William Collins' dream of knowledge for all began with the publication of his 'rst book in 1819. A self-educated mill worker, he not only enriched millions of lives, but also founded a ‚ourishing publishing house. Today, staying true to this spirit, Collins books are packed with inspiration, innovation, and practical expertise. They place you at the centre of a world of possibility and give you exactly what you need to explore it.

Language is the key to this exploration, and at the heart of Collins Dictionaries is language as it is really used. New words, phrases, and meanings spring up every day, and all of them are captured and analysed by the Collins Word Web. Constantly updated, and with over 2.5 billion entries, this living language resource is unique to our dictionaries. Words are tools for life. And a Collins Dictionary makes them work for you.

Collins. Do more.

CONTENTS

FOREWORD FOR LANGUAGE TEACHERS

The *Easy Learning Irish Grammar* is designed to be used with both young and adult learners, as a group reference book to complement your course book during classes, or as a recommended text for self-study and homework/coursework.

The text specifically targets learners from *ab initio* to intermediate or GCSE Level, and Ordinary Level at Leaving Certificate and therefore its structural content and vocabulary have been matched to these levels.

The approach aims to develop knowledge and understanding of grammar and your learners' ability to apply it by:

- defining parts of speech at the start of each major section with examples in English to clarify concepts
- providing clear explanations of grammar terms both within the text and in the Glossary
- illustrating all points with examples (and their translations) based on topics and contexts which are relevant to beginner and intermediate course content

The text helps you develop positive attitudes to grammar learning in your classes by:

- giving clear, easy-to-follow explanations
- highlighting useful **Tips** to deal with common difficulties
- summarizing **Key points** at the end of sections to consolidate learning

INTRODUCTION FOR STUDENTS

Whether you are starting to learn Irish for the very first time, brushing up on topics you have studied in class, or revising for your exams, the *Easy Learning Irish Grammar* is here to help. This easy-to-use guide takes you through all the basics you will need to speak and understand modern, everyday Irish.

Newcomers can sometimes struggle with the technical terms they come across when they start to explore the grammar of a new language. The *Easy Learning Irish Grammar* explains how to get to grips with the parts of speech you will need to know using simple language.

The text is divided into sections, each dealing with a particular area of grammar. Each section can be studied individually, as numerous cross-references in the text point you to relevant points in other sections of the book for further information.

The major sections begin with an explanation of the area of grammar covered on the following pages:

What is a verb?
A **verb** is a 'doing' word which describes what someone or something does, what someone or something is, or what happens to them, for example, *run*, *cry*, *jump*.

Each grammar point in the text is followed by simple examples of real Irish, complete with English translations, helping you understand the rules. Underlining has been used in examples throughout the text to highlight the grammatical point being explained:

➤**Nár** is only used in the past tense with regular verbs and with the irregular verbs **beir** *grab*, **clois/cluin** *hear*, **ith** *eat*, **tabhair** *give*, **tar** *come*. **Nár** aspirates but has no effect on verbs beginning with vowels:

na scoláirí nár bhris na rialacha	the students **who didn't break** the rules
sin an buachaill nár oscail a bhronntanas	that's the boy **who didn't open** his present

In Irish, as with any language, there are certain pitfalls which have to be avoided. **Tips** and **Information** notes throughout the text are useful reminders of the things that often trip learners up:

> ## Típ
> **-a** is added to adjectives that end in a consonant preceded by **a, á, o, ó, u** or **ú**
> **-e** is added to adjectives that end in a consonant preceded by **e, é, i** or **í**

Key points sum up all the important facts about a particular area of grammar, to save you time when you are revising and help you focus on the main grammatical points:

> ### KEY POINTS
> ✔ When we are saying what the date is, we use the **ordinal numbers**.
> ✔ We also must use a special form of the months when saying what date it is.

Finally, the supplement at the end of the book contains **Verb Tables**, where many important Irish verbs (both regular and irregular) are declined in full. Examples show you how to use these verbs in your own work. If you are unsure of how a verb conjugates in Irish, you can look up the **Verbs Index** on pages 26–31 to find either the conjugation of the verb itself, or a cross-reference to a model verb, which will show you the patterns that verb follows.

We hope that you will enjoy using the ***Easy Learning Irish Grammar*** and find it useful in the course of your study.

GLOSSARY

ADJECTIVE a word that tells you more about a person or thing, describing their appearance, colour, size or other qualities, for example, *pretty*, *blue*, *big*.

ADVERB a word usually used with verbs, adjectives or other adverbs that gives more information about when, where, how or in what circumstances something happens, for example, *quickly*, *happily*, *now*.

AGREE (to) to change word endings according to whether you are referring to masculine, feminine, singular or plural people or things.

AGREEMENT changing word endings according to whether you are referring to masculine, feminine, singular or plural people or things.

ARTICLE a word like *the* which is used in front of a noun.

CARDINAL NUMBER a number used in counting, for example, *one, seven, ninety*. Compare with **ordinal number**.

COMPARATIVE an adjective or adverb with *-er* on the end of it or *more* or *less* in front of it that is used to compare people, things or actions, for example, *slower, less important, more carefully*.

CONDITIONAL a verb form used to talk about things that would happen or would be true under certain conditions, for example, *I would help you if I could*. It is also used to say what you would like or need, for example, *Could you give me the bill?*

CONJUGATE (to) to give a verb different endings according to whether you are referring to *I, you, they* and so on, and according to whether you are referring to past, present or future, for example, *have, she had, they will have*.

CONJUGATION a group of verbs which have the same endings as each other or change according to the same pattern.

CONJUNCTION a word such as *and, because* or *but* that links two words or phrases of a similar type or two parts of a sentence, for example, *Diane and I have been friends for years.; I left because I was bored.*

CONSONANT a letter of the alphabet which is not a vowel, for example, *b*, *f*, *m*, *s*, *v* etc. Compare with **VOWEL**.

DEFINITE ARTICLE the word *the*. Compare with **indefinite article**.

DEMONSTRATIVE ADJECTIVE one of the words *this*, *that*, *these* and *those* used with a noun to point out a particular person or thing, for example, <u>*this*</u> woman, <u>*that*</u> dog.

DEMONSTRATIVE PRONOUN one of the words *this*, *that*, *these* and *those* used instead of a noun to point out people or things, for example, <u>*That*</u> looks fun.

DIRECT OBJECT a noun referring to the person or thing affected by the action described by a verb, for example, *She wrote <u>her name.</u>; I shut <u>the window</u>*. Compare with **indirect object**.

ENDING a form added to a verb, for example, *go* → <u>*goes*</u>, and to adjectives and nouns depending on whether they refer to masculine, feminine, singular or plural things.

FEMININE a form of noun, pronoun or adjective that is used to refer to a living being, thing or idea that is not classed as masculine.

FUTURE a verb tense used to talk about something that will happen or will be true.

GENDER whether a noun, pronoun or adjective is feminine or masculine.

IMPERATIVE the form of a verb used when giving orders and instructions, for example, *Shut the door!; Sit down!; Don't go!*

INDIRECT QUESTION used to tell someone else about a question and introduced by a verb such as *ask*, *tell* or *wonder*, for example, *He asked me what the time was; I wonder who he is.*

INFINITIVE the form of the verb with *to* in front of it and without any endings added, for example, *to walk, to have, to be, to go.* Compare with **stem**.

INTERROGATIVE ADJECTIVE a question word used with a noun to ask *who?*, *what?* or *which?* for example, <u>*What*</u> instruments do you play?; <u>*Which*</u> shoes do you like?

INTERROGATIVE PRONOUN one of the words *who*, *whose*, *whom*, *what* and *which* when they are used instead of a noun to ask questions, for example, _What's happening?_; _Who's coming?_

INVARIABLE used to describe a form which does not change.

IRREGULAR VERB a verb whose forms do not follow a general pattern or the normal rules. Compare with **regular verb**.

MASCULINE a form of noun, pronoun or adjective that is used to refer to a living being, thing or idea that is not classed as feminine.

NEGATIVE a question or statement which contains a word such as _not_, _never_ or _nothing_, and is used to say that something is not happening, is not true or is absent, for example, _I never eat meat_; _Don't you love me?_

NOUN a 'naming' word for a living being, thing or idea, for example, _woman_, _desk_, _happiness_, _Andrew_.

NUMBER used to say how many things you are referring to or where something comes in a sequence. See also **ordinal number** and **cardinal number**.

OBJECT a noun or pronoun which refers to a person or thing that is affected by the action described by the verb. Compare with **direct object**, **indirect object** and **subject**.

OBJECT a word such as _me_, _him_, _us_ and _them_ which is used instead of a noun to stand in for the person or thing most directly affected by the action described by the verb.

ORDINAL NUMBER a number used to indicate where something comes in an order or sequence, for example, _first_, _fifth_, _sixteenth_. Compare with **cardinal number**.

PART OF SPEECH a word class, for example, _noun_, _verb_, _adjective_, _preposition_, _pronoun_.

PASSIVE a form of the verb that is used when the subject of the verb is the person or thing that is affected by the action, for example, _we were told_.

PAST PARTICIPLE a verb form which is used to form perfect and pluperfect tenses and passives, for example, _watched_, _swum_. Some past participles are also used as adjectives, for example, _a broken watch_.

PERFECT one of the verb tenses used to talk about the past, especially about actions that took place and were completed in the past.

PERSON one of the three classes: the first person (*I*, *we*), the second person (*you* singular and *you* plural), and the third person (*he*, *she*, *it* and *they*).

PERSONAL PRONOUN one of the group of words including *I*, *you* and *they* which are used to refer to yourself, the people you are talking to, or the people or things you are talking about.

PLURAL the form of a word which is used to refer to more than one person or thing. Compare with **singular**.

POSSESSIVE ADJECTIVE one of the words *my*, *your*, *his*, *her*, *its*, *our* or *their*, used with a noun to show that one person or thing belongs to another.

POSSESSIVE PRONOUN one of the words *mine*, *yours*, *hers*, *his*, *ours* or *theirs*, used instead of a noun to show that one person or thing belongs to another.

PREPOSITION a word such as *at*, *for*, *with*, *into* or *from*, which is usually followed by a noun, pronoun or, in English, a word ending in *-ing*. Prepositions show how people and things relate to the rest of the sentence, for example, *She's <u>at</u> home; a tool <u>for</u> cutting grass; It's <u>from</u> David*.

PRESENT a verb form used to talk about what is true at the moment, what happens regularly, and what is happening now, for example, *I'<u>m</u> a student; I <u>travel</u> to college by train; I'<u>m studying</u> languages*.

PRONOUN a word which you use instead of a noun, when you do not need or want to name someone or something directly, for example, *it*, *you*, *none*.

REFLEXIVE PRONOUN a word ending in *-self* or *-selves*, such as *myself* or *themselves*, which refers back to the subject, for example, *He hurt <u>himself</u>.; Take care of <u>yourself</u>.*

REGULAR VERB a verb whose forms follow a general pattern or the normal rules. Compare with **irregular verb**.

RELATIVE PRONOUN a word such as *that*, *who* or *which*, when it is used to link two parts of a sentence together.

SENTENCE a group of words which usually has a verb and a subject. In writing, a sentence has a capital letter at the beginning and a full stop, question mark or exclamation mark at the end.

SINGULAR the form of a word which is used to refer to one person or thing. Compare with **plural**.

STEM the form of the verb without any endings added to it, for example, *walk, have, be, go*. Compare with **infinitive**.

SUBJECT the noun or pronoun in a sentence or phrase that refers to the person or thing that does the action described by the verb or is in the state described by the verb, for example, *My cat doesn't drink milk*. Compare with **object**.

SUBJECT PRONOUN a word such as *I, he, she* and *they* which carries out the action described by the verb. Pronouns stand in for nouns when it is clear who is being talked about, for example, *My brother isn't here at the moment. He'll be back in an hour*. Compare with **object pronoun**.

SUBJUNCTIVE a verb form used in certain circumstances to express some sort of feeling, or to show doubt about whether something will happen or whether something is true. It is only used occasionally in modern English, for example, *If I were you, I wouldn't bother.; So be it*.

SUPERLATIVE an adjective or adverb with *-est* on the end of it or *most* or *least* in front of it that is used to compare people, things or actions, for example, *thinnest, most quickly, least interesting*.

SYLLABLE consonant + vowel units that make up the sounds of a word, for example, *ca-the-dral* (3 syllables), *im-po-ssi-ble* (4 syllables).

TENSE the form of a verb which shows whether you are referring to the past, present or future.

VERB a 'doing' word which describes what someone or something does, what someone or something is, or what happens to them, for example, *be, sing, live*.

VOWEL one of the letters *a, e, i, o* or *u*. Compare with **consonant**.

Grammar

ASPIRATION AND ECLIPSES

1 Aspiration

> **What is aspiration?**
> Aspiration is when we place the letter **h** after the initial consonant of words in Irish. There are certain consonants that cannot be aspirated, and vowels are never aspirated. Aspiration causes the pronunciation to change, and the pronunciation depends on whether the consonant is **broad** (followed by *a, o, u*) or **slender** (followed by *i, e*).
>
> The letters **b, c, d, f, g, m, p, s, t** can all be aspirated.

1.1 When do we aspirate nouns?

➤ After the article **an**:

- when a masculine noun is in the genitive case:

  ceann an chapaill   *the horse's head*

  obair an fheirmeora   *the farmer's work*

- when a feminine noun is in its normal form:

  D'imigh an bhean.   *The woman left.*

  Dún an fhuinneog!   *Close the window!*

⇨ The Contents page at the beginning of the book and the Main Index on page 233 show where to find more information on grammar concepts apppearing in this chapter.

➤ In the vocative case – both singular and plural:

A Sheáin, tar anseo!	*Seán, come here!*
A bhuachaillí, ná déanaigí sin!	*Boys, don't do that!*

➤ After the following prepositions: **ar** *on*, **de** *from*, **do** *to*, **faoi** *under*, **idir** *between*, **mar** *as*, **ó** *from*, **roimh** *before*, **thar** *over*, **trí** *through*, **um** *about*:

ar Sheán	*on Seán*
de Mháire	*from Máire*
do bhuachaillí	*for boys*
faoi chrann	*under a tree*
mar dhuine	*as a person*
ó mhaidin	*from morning*
roimh Shamhain	*before Hallowe'en*
um Cháisc	*around Easter*

- The preposition **gan** *without* aspirates in general use, but not when words begin with **d, f, s, t**:

gan mhoill	*without delay*

➤ After **den** *from the*, **don** *to the* and **sa** *in the*:

Thit sé den chrann.	*He fell from the tree.*
Thug mé cuidiú don bhuachaill.	*I gave help to the boy.*
Tá an cóta sa chófra.	*The coat is in the cupboard.*

➤ In Ulster Irish after **ar an** *on the*, **ag an** *at the*, **as an** *from the*, **faoin** *under the*, **tríd an** *through the*, **ón** *from the*, **leis an** *with the*:

Chuaigh Aoibh tríd an pháirc.	*Aoibh went through the park.*
Beidh Orlaith ag ceol ar an chlár.	*Orlaith will be singing on the programme.*

➤After the possessive adjectives **mo** *my*, **do** *your*, **a** *his*:

Is í Michelle mo bheanchéile.	*Michelle is my wife.*
Cá bhfuil do chóta?	*Where is your coat?*
Tá a chara iontach tinn.	*His friend is very sick.*

➤After **aon** *one*, **d(h)á** *two* and **céad** *first*:

aon fhear amháin	*one man*
dhá bhróg	*two shoes*
an dá bhliain sin	*those two years*
an chéad chuid den scéal	*the first part of the story*

➤After **trí** *three*, **ceithre** *four*, **cúig** *five*, **sé** *six*:

trí bhó	*three cows*
ceithre chapall	*four horses*
sé mhíle	*six miles*

➤After the copula in the past tense and the conditional, **ba, ar gur, níor, nár**:

Ba bhád beag é.	*It was a small boat.*
Níor chaillteanas mór é.	*It wasn't a huge loss.*

➤If the noun is the second part of a compound word:

seanfhear	*an old man*
dea-thoil	*good will*

➤If the noun is a proper noun in the genitive:

Scoil Phádraig	*Patrick's school*
in aice Bhéal Feirste	*beside Belfast*

➤If the noun is the first word of a phrase in the genitive:

scéal mhuintir na hÉireann	*the story of the people of Ireland*

➤If the noun is in the genitive after a noun that ends in a slender consonant (if the letter *i* appears in front of it):

fir cheoil	*music men*

1.2   When do we aspirate adjectives?

➤When the adjective describes a feminine noun in its normal form:

D'imigh an ghirseach bheag.	*The small girl left.*
Cá bhfuil an leabharlann phoiblí?	*Where is the public library?*

➤When the adjective describes a noun in the genitive singular:

hata an fhir mhóir	*the big man's hat*
doras an tsiopa bhig	*the door of the small shop*

➤When the adjective describes a noun in the plural, if the noun ends in a slender consonant:

Tá scamaill dhubha sa spear.	*There are black clouds in the sky.*
Cuir na cupáin ghlana sa chófra.	*Put the clean cups in the cupboard.*

➤ If the numbers 2–19 precede the noun, the adjective following them is aspirated:

dhá chapall bhána	*two white horses*
seacht mbó mhóra	*seven large cows*

➤ After **beirt** two:

beirt fhear mhóra	*two big men*

1.3 When do we aspirate verbs?

➤ In the past tense and in the conditional:

Chaill sé a mhála inné.	*He lost his bag yesterday.*
Thiocfadh sé dá mb'fhéidir leis.	*He would come if he could.*

➤ After the particles **ní, níor, ar, nár, cár, má**:

Ní fheicim é.	*I don't see him.*
Níor dhíol sé as.	*He didn't pay for it.*

➤ After the relative pronoun in direct clauses:

an fear a dhíolann tithe	*the man who sells houses*

➤ After **cad é a** what, **cathain a** when, **cé a** who, **cén uair a** when, **conas a** how, **céard a** what, **mar a** as, **nuair a** when:

Cé a dhéanfaidh é?	*Who will do it?*
Cén uair a thiocfaidh sé?	*When will he come?*

2 Eclipses

What are eclipses?

An eclipse is the placing of a letter in front of another letter.
The eclipsing letter then becomes the dominant sound.
Each letter in Irish which can be eclipsed has its own eclipsing letter. The eclipsing letter is highlighted in bold.

mb   **g**c   **n**d   **bh**f   **n**g   **b**p   **d**t

All vowels are eclipsed by **n-**, except when the noun begins with a capital letter: **ár n-athair** *our father*, but **ár nUachtarán** *our president*.

2.1 When do we eclipse nouns?

➤ In Connaught and Munster Irish nouns are eclipsed after **ar an** *on the*, **ag an** *at the*, **as an** *from the*, **faoin** *under the*, **tríd an** *through the*, **ón** *from the*:

ar an gcapall	*on the horse*
as an mbád	*from the boat*

➤ In the genitive plural after the article **na**:

tormán na dtonn	*the sound of the waves*

➤ After the preposition **i**:

i mbliana	*this year*
i bponc	*in trouble*
i nDoire	*in Derry*

➤After the possessive adjectives **ár** *our*, **bhur** *your* (plural) and **a** *their*:

> **Déanfaimid ár ndícheall.** *We will do our best.*
>
> **Chaill sibh bhur gciall.** *You lost your senses.*

➤After **seacht** *seven*, **ocht** *eight*, **naoi** *nine* and **deich** *ten*:

> **seacht mbliana** *seven years*
>
> **deich n-asal** *ten donkeys*

2.2 When do we eclipse verbs?

➤After **an, nach, go** and **cá**:

> **An bhfaca tú an fear sin?** *Did you see that man?*
>
> **Nach dtuigeann tú an cheist?** *Don't you understand the question?*

➤After **dá** *if* and **mura** *if not*:

> **Dá bhfeicfeá é bheadh iontas ort.** *If you saw it you would be amazed.*
>
> **Mura n-ólfaidh seisean é, ólfaidh mise é.** *If he doesn't drink it I will drink it.*

➤After the indirect particle **a**:

> **an buachaill a bhfuair a athair bás** *the boy whose father died*

NOUNS

What is a noun?
A **noun** is a 'naming' word for a living being, thing or idea, for example, *boy*, *love*, *Seán*.

1 Overview of nouns

➤ Nouns in Irish have different genders. They are either masculine or feminine. Grammatical gender in Irish is not connected with biological gender, as we see with the word **cailín** *a girl*, which is a masculine noun!

➤ Nouns in Irish form their plurals by adding to the noun OR by changing it internally:

gasúr *a boy*	**gasú<u>i</u>r** *boys*
cailín *a girl*	**cailín<u>í</u>** *girls*

➤ Nouns in Irish can be aspirated or eclipsed. This is explained in chapter 1.

cófra *a cupboard*	**sa c<u>h</u>ófra** *in the cupboard*
gluaisteán *a car*	**ar an <u>n</u>gluaisteán** *on the car*

➤ Nouns in Irish can have **t-** placed in front of them:

arán *bread*	**an <u>t</u>-arán** *the bread*

➤ Nouns in Irish can have **h-** placed in front of them:

an áit *the place*	**na <u>h</u>áiteanna** *the places*

➤ The Irish word for *the* is either **an** or **na**, depending on whether the noun following is singular or plural, or a feminine noun in the genitive case:

an scoil *the school*	**na scoileanna** *the schools*
an pháirc *the field*	**lár na páirce** *the middle of the field*

Típ

There is no word for *a* in Irish. So, the word **bean** means both *a woman* and *woman*:

Chonaic mé bean.   *I saw a woman.*

2   The common form of nouns

Look at this sentence:

D'ith an fear an dinnéar.   *The man ate the dinner.*

There are two nouns in this sentence – **an fear** *'the man'* and **an dinnéar** *'the dinner'*. *The man* is the **subject** of the sentence (the person, place or thing which carries out the action) and *the dinner* is the **object** of the sentence (a person, place or thing involved in the action, but which doesn't carry it out). When a noun is the **subject** or **object** of a sentence, we say that the noun is in the **common form**, whether it is singular or plural.

i   We can tell whether a noun is masculine or feminine by its ending.

2.1 Masculine nouns and their plural in the common form

There are 3 main groups of masculine nouns:

➤ **Group 1:** Nouns that end in a **broad consonant** (a consonant or group of consonants which has *a/á, o/ó* or *u/ú* before it).

- Their plural is formed by placing *i* before the last consonant or by changing **ach** to **aigh**.

- **An** does not make any difference to the start of a noun beginning with a consonant, but places *t-* before a vowel at the start of the noun.

- **Na** does not make any difference to the start of a noun beginning with a consonant, but places *h-* before a vowel at the start of a plural noun.

Singular		Plural	
bád a boat	*an bád* the boat	*báid* boats	*na báid* the boats
cosán a footpath	*an cosán* the footpath	*cosáin* footpaths	*na cosáin* the footpaths
cnoc a hill	*an cnoc* the hill	*cnoic* hills	*na cnoic* the hills
asal a donkey	*an t-asal* the donkey	*asail* donkeys	*na hasail* the donkeys
marcach a jockey	*an marcach* the jockey	*marcaigh* jockeys	*na marcaigh* the jockeys

➤**Group 2:** Nouns that indicate professions and end in *-éir, -eoir, -óir*.

- Their plural is formed by placing *í* at the end of the word.

- *An* does not have any effect if the noun starts with a consonant, but places *t-* before a vowel at the start of a noun.

- *Na* does not have any effect if the noun starts with a consonant, but places *h-* before a vowel at the start of a plural noun.

Singular		Plural	
feirmeoir a farmer	*an feirmeoir* the farmer	*feirmeoirí* farmers	*na feirmeoirí* the farmers
bádóir a boatman	*an bádóir* the boatman	*bádóirí* boatmen	*na bádóirí* the boatmen
siopadóir a shopkeeper	*an siopadóir* the shopkeeper	*siopadóirí* shopkeepers	*na siopadóirí* the shopkeepers
aisteoir an actor	*an t-aisteoir* the actor	*aisteoirí* actors	*na haisteoirí* the actors

➤**Group 3:** Nouns that end in **-ín**.

- Their plural is formed by placing **í** at the end of the word.

- **An** does not have any effect if the noun starts with a consonant, but places **t-** before a vowel at the start of a noun.

- **Na** does not have any effect if the noun starts with a consonant, but places **h-** before a vowel at the start of a plural noun.

Singular		Plural	
cailín a girl	*an cailín* the girl	*cailíní* girls	*na cailíní* the girls
sicín a chicken	*an sicín* the chicken	*sicíní* chickens	*na sicíní* the chickens
coinín a rabbit	*an coinín* the rabbit	*coiníní* rabbits	*na coiníní* the rabbits
ispín a sausage	*an t-ispín* the sausage	*ispíní* sausages	*na hispíní* the sausages

2.2 Feminine nouns and their plural in the common form

There are 3 main groups of feminine nouns:

➤**Group 1:** Nouns that end in **-óg** or **-eog**.

- Their plural is formed by adding **a** to the end of the word.

- **An** causes the initial consonant of a noun to be aspirated, but has no effect if the noun starts with a vowel.

- **Na** does not have any effect if the noun starts with a consonant but places **h-** before a vowel at the start of a plural noun.

Singular		Plural	
bróg *a shoe*	**an bhróg** *the shoe*	**bróga** *shoes*	**na bróga** *the shoes*
fuinneog *a window*	**an fhuinneog** *the window*	**fuinneoga** *windows*	**na fuinneoga** *the windows*
ordóg *a thumb*	**an ordóg** *the thumb*	**ordóga** *thumbs*	**na hordóga** *the thumbs*

➤**Group 2:** Nouns that end in a **slender consonant** (a consonant which has *i* before it).

- Their plural is formed by adding *eanna* or *eacha*.

- *An* causes the initial consonant of a noun to be aspirated, but has no effect on words beginning with vowels.

- *Na* does not have any effect if the noun starts with a consonant but places *h-* before a vowel at the start of a plural noun.

Singular		Plural	
páirc *a field*	**an pháirc** *the field*	**páirceanna** *fields*	**na páirceanna** *the fields*
áit *place*	**an áit** *the place*	**áiteanna** *places*	**na háiteanna** *the places*

➤**Group 3:** Nouns that end in *-lann* and refer to a place.

- Their plural is formed by adding *-a*.

- *An* causes the initial consonant of a noun to be aspirated, but does nothing to a noun beginning with a vowel.

- **Na** does not have any effect if the noun starts with a consonant but places **h-** before a vowel at the start of a plural noun.

Singular		Plural	
pictiúrlann *a cinema*	**an p̲h̲ictiúrlann** *the cinema*	**pictiúrlanna̲** *cinemas*	**na pictiúrlanna̲** *the cinemas*
amharclann *a theatre*	**an amharclann** *the theatre*	**amharclanna̲** *theatres*	**na h̲amharclanna̲** *the theatres*

⇨ See chapter 1 for further information on aspiration.

> *Típ*
>
> The names of a lot of countries, continents and rivers are feminine:
>
> | **An Fhrainc** | *France* |
> |---|---|
> | **An Rúis** | *Russia* |
> | **An Eoraip** | *Europe* |
> | **An Fheabhail** | *The Foyle* |
>
> The names of languages are mostly feminine:
>
> | **An Ghaeilge** | *Irish* |
> |---|---|
> | **An Spáinnis** | *Spanish* |

3 Other forms of nouns

Nouns also appear in Irish in a number of other forms, or cases as they are called.

> **Cases**
> A **case** is a change in a noun which shows its relationship to other words in the sentence. In English this happens most often when **'s** is added to a noun to show that the noun owns something:
>
> *Claire's bike; the team's goalkeeper; the city's history*

There are more cases in Irish than in English.

3.1 Nouns in the vocative case

A noun is in the **vocative case** when it is used to name the person or thing that is addressed. To form the vocative case, we place *a* before the noun and aspirate it. With masculine names ending in a broad consonant, we both aspirate and place *i* before the last consonant.

Tar anseo, a chara.	*Come here, friend.*
Ná déan sin, a Dhiarmaid.	*Don't do that, Diarmaid.*
A chailíní, ná bígí mall.	*Girls, don't be late.*

3.2 Nouns in the dative case

▶A noun is put into the **dative case** if it comes after the following prepositions:

ag	ar	as	chuig	de
at	*on*	*from*	*to*	*off*
do	faoi	go	i	le
to	*under*	*to*	*in*	*with*
ó	thart	trí	um	
from	*around*	*through*	*around*	

➤ Some of these prepositions cause aspiration to the beginning of words.

> **Tá gaineamh ar thrá.**   *There is sand on a beach.*

➤ When these prepositions are placed before nouns which have **an** in front of them, **aspiration** or **eclipses** can also occur. This is discussed further in the chapter on Prepositions.

> **Bhí fear ag an fhuinneog.**   *There was a man at the window.*
>
> **Bhí fear an an bhfuinneog.**   *There was a man at the window.*

3.3 Nouns in the genitive case

➤ This is the form of the noun which shows possession, like the 's or *of* in English. Where two nouns occur together in Irish, the second is usually in the genitive.

> **teach Sheáin**   <u>Seán's</u> house
>
> **muintir na háite**   the people <u>of the place</u>
>
> **cupán tae**   a cup <u>of tea</u>

➤ The genitive is used after **compound prepositions**, which are prepositions made up of more than one word. This is discussed further in the chapter on Prepositions.

    *ar fud **na cathrach***   *throughout the city*

    *os comhair **an tí***   *opposite the house*

➤The genitive is used after **ag + verbal noun**, which is a noun derived from the verb. This corresponds to -*ing* words in English, like *cleaning*, *working* etc.

    ag glanadh na fuinneoige   *cleaning the window*

    ag scríobh leabhair   *writing a book*

➤The genitive is used after the following:

timpeall	*around*	**timpeall an tí** *around the house*
chun	*to*	**chun na Fraince** *to France*
trasna	*across*	**trasna na habhann** *across the river*
cois	*beside*	**cois na farraige** *beside the sea*
mórán	*a lot of*	**mórán airgid** *a lot of money*
beagán	*a small amount of*	**beagán céille** *a small amount of sense*
a lán	*a lot of*	**a lán daoine** *a lot of people*

4 Forming the genitive case

> How we form the genitive of nouns depends on whether they are masculine or feminine, and their endings.

4.1 Masculine nouns in the genitive

➤**Group 1:** Nouns that end in a **broad consonant** (a consonant or group of consonants which has *a/á, o/ó* or *u/ú* before it) or nouns that end in *éar/ear*.

- The genitive is formed by placing *i* before the last consonant, or by changing *-ach* to *-aigh* or *-each* to *-igh*.

- If the noun starts with a consonant, *an* causes aspiration. There is no effect if the noun starts with a vowel.

an bád the boat	*fear an bháid* the man of the boat
an cosán the footpath	*bun an chosáin* the bottom of the footpath
an cnoc the hill	*barr an chnoic* the top of the hill
an t-asal the donkey	*cluasa an asail* the donkey\ears
an marcach the jockey	*capall an mharcaigh* the jockey's horse
an fear the man	*hata an fhir* the man's hat

➤**Group 2:** Nouns that indicate professions and end in *-éir, -eoir, -óir*.

- Their genitive is formed by changing *-éir* to *-éara*, *-eoir* to *-eora* and *-óir* to *-óra*.

- If the noun starts with a consonant *an* causes aspiration. It has no effect if the noun starts with a vowel.

an feirmeoir *the farmer*	*teach an fheirmeora* *the farmer's house*
an bádóir *the boatman*	*bean an bhádóra* *the boatman's wife*
an t-aisteoir *the actor*	*gluaisteán an aisteora* *the actor's car*

➤**Group 3:** Nouns that end in *-ín*.

- The genitive is the same as the common form.

- If the noun starts with a consonant *an* causes aspiration. There is no effect if the noun starts with a vowel.

an cailín *the girl*	*gúna an chailín* *the girl's dress*
an coinín *the rabbit*	*poll an choinín* *the rabbit's hole*
an ispín *the sausage*	*blas an ispín* *the taste of the sausage*

4.2 Feminine nouns and the genitive

➤**Group 1:** Nouns that end in *-óg* or *-eog*.

- Their genitive is formed by changing *-óg* to *-óige* and *-eog* to *-eoige*.

- *An* changes to *na* in the genitive singular. It has no effect if the noun starts with a consonant, but causes *h* to be added if the noun starts with a vowel.

an bhróg the shoe	Iall na bróige the shoelace
an fhuinneog the window	gloine na fuinneoige the glass of the window
an ordóg the thumb	barr na hordóige the top of the thumb

➤**Group 2:** Nouns that end in a **slender consonant** (a consonant which has *i* before it).

- Their genitive is formed by adding *-e*.

- *An* changes to *na* in the genitive singular. It has no effect if the noun starts with a consonant, but causes *h* to be added if the noun starts with a vowel.

an pháirc the field	lár na páirce the middle of the field
an áit the place	muintir na háite the people of the place

➤**Group 3:** Nouns that end in *-lann* and refer to a place.

- Their genitive is formed by changing *-lann* to *-lainne*.

- *An* changes to *na* in the genitive singular. It has no effect if the noun starts with a consonant, but causes *h* to be added if the noun starts with a vowel.

an phictiúrlann the cinema	*doras na pictiúrlainne* the door of the cinema
an amharclann the theatre	*úinéir na hamharclainne* the owner of the theatre

KEY POINTS

✔ There is no word for *a* in Irish.
✔ The word for *the* is either **an** or **na**.
✔ Plurals of nouns in Irish can be formed by an internal change, or by adding a sound to the end of the noun.
✔ Nouns in Irish have different forms called cases.
✔ We can tell whether a noun is masculine or feminine by its ending.
✔ Nouns in Irish can be aspirated or eclipsed.

PRONOUNS

What is a pronoun?
A **pronoun** is a word you use instead of a noun, when you do not need or want to name someone or something directly, for example, *it, you, none*.

There are two main types of pronoun in Irish:

➤ **Personal pronouns** such as *I, you, he, her* and *they*, which are used to refer to yourself, the person you are talking to, or other people and things. They can be either **subject pronouns** (*I, you, he* and so on) or **direct object pronouns** (*him, her, them* and so on).

➤ **Prepositional pronouns** such as *with me, on him, to them*. These appear in Irish as single words.

1 Personal pronouns: subject

What is a subject pronoun?
A **subject pronoun** is a word such as *I, he, she* and *they*, which performs the action expressed by the verb. Pronouns stand in for nouns when it is clear who is being talked about, for example, *My sister wasn't here yesterday. She was at school.*

1.1 Using subject pronouns

Here are the Irish subject pronouns:

Singular	Meaning	Plural	Meaning
mé	I	**muid/sinn**	we
tú	you	**sibh**	you
sé	he it (masculine)	**siad**	they
sí	she it (feminine)		

Chonaic <u>mé</u> an gasúr sin.	I saw that boy.
Beidh <u>sí</u> anseo amárach.	She will be here tomorrow.
Druideann <u>siad</u> an geata gach lá ar a sé a chlog.	They close the gate every day at 6 o'clock.

1.2 Subject pronouns in synthetic forms

When the subject pronoun is incorporated into the verb and appears as one word this is called a synthetic form.

Ithim	I eat
Cheannaíomar	We bought
Déanfaimid	We shall make

⇨ For more information on the endings we should add to verbs which include the subject pronoun, see chapter 5 on Verbs.

1.3 *sé* and *sí* meaning 'it'

In English we generally refer to things (such as *car*, *pen*, *cup*) only as *it*. In Irish, **sé** (meaning *he*, *it*) and **sí** (meaning *she*, *it*) are used to talk about nouns. We use **sé** for **masculine nouns** and **sí** for **feminine nouns**.

An peann is a masculine noun:

> **Tá an peann ar an tábla.**   *The pen is on the table.*
>
> **Tá sé ar an tábla.**   *It is on the table.*

An leabharlann is a feminine noun:

> **Tá an leabharlann thall ansin.**   *The library is over there.*
>
> **Tá sí thall ansin.**   *It is over there.*

⇨   For more information on masculine and feminine nouns, see chapter 2 on Nouns.

1.4 Emphatic forms of subject pronouns

In English, to emphasise words, we tend to raise our voice: *HE isn't to blame.* In Irish we do not do this. Instead we use special emphatic forms of the subject pronouns.

Here are the emphatic subject pronouns in Irish:

Singular	Meaning	Plural	Meaning
mise	*I*	**muidne/sinne**	*we*
tusa	*you*	**sibhse**	*you*
seisean	*he* *it* (masculine)	**siadsan**	*they*
síse	*she* *it* (feminine)		

KEY POINTS

✔ The Irish subject pronouns are **mé, tú, sé, sí** in the singular, and **muid/sinn, sibh, siad** in the plural.

✔ Subject pronouns can appear as part of the verb.

✔ **sé** and **sí** are used for *it*, depending on whether the noun is masculine or feminine.

2 Personal pronouns: direct object

What is a direct object pronoun?
A **direct object pronoun** is a word such as *me*, *him*, *us* and *them*, which is used instead of the noun to stand in for the person or thing most directly affected by the action expressed by the verb.

2.1 Using direct object pronouns

➤ Direct object pronouns stand in for nouns when it is clear who or what is being talked about, and save having to repeat the noun:

> *I will not see the boys. Will you see <u>them</u>?*

> *Did you see that man? No, I didn't see <u>him</u>.*

➤ Here are the Irish direct object pronouns:

Singular	Meaning	Plural	Meaning
mé	me	**muid/sinn**	us
thú	you	**sibh**	you
é	him it	**iad**	them
í	her it		

> **Chonaic Mairéad <u>thú</u>.**   *Mairéad saw <u>you</u>.*

> **Íosfaimid <u>iad</u>.**   *We'll eat <u>them</u>.*

> **Spreagann m'athair <u>mé</u>.**   *My father inspires <u>me</u>.*

2.2 é and í meaning 'it'

In English we generally refer to things (such as *car, pen, cup*) only as *it*. In Irish, *é* (meaning *him, it*) and *í* (meaning *her, it*) are used to talk about nouns. We use *é* for **masculine nouns** and *í* for **feminine nouns.**

An cupán is a masculine noun:

Bhris Rhiannon an cupán.	*Rhiannon broke the cup.*
Bhris Rhiannon é.	*Rhiannon broke it.*

An phictiúrlann is a feminine noun:

Osclóidh an tUachtarán an phictiúrlann.	*The President will open the cinema.*
Osclóidh an tUachtarán í.	*The President will open it.*

⇨ For more information on masculine and feminine nouns, see chapter 2 on Nouns.

2.3 Emphatic forms of object pronouns

In English, to emphasise words, we tend to raise our voice: *I like HIM, but not HER*. In Irish we do not do this. Instead we use emphatic forms of the object pronouns.

The emphatic form in Irish:

Singular	Meaning	Plural	Meaning
mise	*me*	**muidne/sinne**	*us*
thusa	*you*	**sibhse**	*you*
eisean	*him* *it (masculine)*	**iadsan**	*them*
ise	*her* *it (feminine)*		

KEY POINTS

✔ The Irish direct object pronouns are **mé, thú, é, í** in the singular, and **muid/sinn, sibh, iad** in the plural.

✔ **é** and **í** are used for *it*, depending on whether the noun is masculine or feminine.

3 Prepositional pronouns

> **What is a prepositional pronoun?**
> A **prepositional pronoun** is a preposition, such as *on*, *with*, *to*, combined with a pronoun. In English, this is very straightforward: we simply say, *on me*, *with him*, *to them*, etc.

➤Unlike in English, prepositional pronouns appear in Irish as one word. If we want to say, for example, *with me*, we do not say **le** *with* + **mé** *me*, but instead we use a synthetic form: **liom** *with me*.

➤Here are the Irish prepositional pronouns:

Prep.	me	you	him	her	us	you	them
ag *at*	*agam*	*agat*	*aige*	*aici*	*againn*	*agaibh*	*acu*
ar *on*	*orm*	*ort*	*air*	*uirthi*	*orainn*	*oraibh*	*orthu*
as *out of*	*asam*	*asat*	*as*	*aisti*	*asainn*	*asaibh*	*astu*
chuig *to*	*chugam*	*chugat*	*chuige*	*chuici*	*chugainn*	*chugaibh*	*chucu*
de *from*	*díom*	*díot*	*de*	*di*	*dínn*	*díbh*	*díobh*
do *to*	*dom*	*duit*	*dó*	*di*	*dúinn*	*daoibh*	*dóibh*
faoi *under*	*fúm*	*fút*	*faoi*	*fúithi*	*fúinn*	*fúibh*	*fúthu*
i *in*	*ionam*	*ionat*	*ann*	*inti*	*ionainn*	*ionaibh*	*iontu*
le *with*	*liom*	*leat*	*leis*	*léi*	*linn*	*libh*	*leo*
ó *from*	*uaim*	*uait*	*uaidh*	*uaithi*	*uainn*	*uaibh*	*uathu*
roimh *before*	*romham*	*romhat*	*roimhe*	*roimpi*	*romhainn*	*romhaibh*	*rompu*

ADJECTIVES

What is an adjective?
An **adjective** is a 'describing' word used to give more information about a noun or pronoun in a sentence, for example, *big*, *small*, *yellow*.

---

1   Attributive adjectives and predicative adjectives

Look at these two sentences:

I. ***Tá an fear <u>mór</u> ag an doras.***	*The big man is at the door.*
II. ***Tá an fear <u>mór</u>.***	*The man is big.*

- In the first sentence the adjective (***mór***) is linked directly to the noun (***fear***). This is an **attributive adjective**.

- In the second sentence the adjective (***mór***) is linked indirectly to the noun (***fear***) using a linking verb (***tá***). This is a **predicative adjective**.

- When an adjective is used directly with a noun, i.e. attributively (as in sentence I.), it must agree with the noun in gender, number and case.

⇨   For more information on gender, number and case of nouns, see chapter 2.

- When an adjective is used indirectly, i.e. predicatively, with a noun (as in sentence II.), it doesn't have to agree with the noun in gender, number or case.

1.1 Attributive adjectives

- The attributive adjective usually comes after the noun in Irish.

- The attributive adjective changes its form depending on the gender, number or case of the noun. This means that:

1. The adjective is masculine if the noun is masculine.

   an gasúr <u>maith</u>   *the good boy*

2. The adjective is feminine if the noun is feminine.

   an ghirseach <u>mhaith</u>   *the good girl*

3. The adjective is singular if the noun is singular.

   an fear <u>mór</u>   *the big man*

4. The adjective is plural if the noun is plural.

   na gasúir <u>mhaithe</u>   *the good boys*

5. The adjective is the dative case if the noun is in the dative.

   leis an fhear <u>mhór</u>/   *with the big man*
   leis an bhfear <u>mór</u>

6. The adjective is in the vocative case if the noun is in the vocative.

   a bhean mhaith   *my good woman*

7. The adjective is in the genitive case if the noun is in the genitive.

   hata an fhir mhóir   *the big man's hat*

1.2 Singular attributive adjectives in the common form

- If the noun is **feminine** the adjective that goes with it is aspirated when possible.

  an bhialann mhaith   *the nice restaurant*

  an chos fhada   *the long foot*

i Vowels can never be aspirated and neither can some consonants. The following cannot be aspirated: **h, j, k, l, n, q, r, v, w, x, y, z, sc, sf, sm, sp, st, sv**

- If the noun is **masculine** nothing is done to the adjective.

  an carr deas   *the nice car*

  an teach costasach   *the expensive house*

1.3 Plural attributive adjectives in the common form

- The adjective is usually made plural by adding **-a** or **-e** to the end of the adjective.

  an buachaill mór   *the big boy*

  na buachaillí móra   *the big boys*

  an oíche mhaith   *the good night*

  na oícheanta maithe   *the good nights*

Típ
-a is added to adjectives that end in a consonant preceded by
a, á, o, ó, u or **ú**

-e is added to adjectives that end in a consonant preceded by
e, é, i or **í**

- If the adjective ends in **-úil** it is changed to **-úla** to make it plural.

  an duine cairdiúil   *the friendly person*

  na daoine cairdiúla   *the friendly people*

- If the adjective ends in **-air** it is changed to **-ra** to make it plural.

  an scrúdú deacair   *the difficult exam*

  na scrúduithe deacra   *the difficult exams*

- The adjective **te** (*warm*) changes to **teo** in the plural.

  an lá te   *the warm day*

  na laethanta teo   *the warm days*

- The adjective **breá** (*fine*) changes to **breátha** in the plural.

  an oíche bhreá   *the fine night*

  na hoícheanta breátha   *the fine nights*

- The adjective **álainn** (*lovely*) changes to **áille** in the plural.

  an cailín álainn *the lovely girl*   **na cailíní áille** *the lovely girls*

ℹ️ There are some adjectives that lose a vowel when they become plural. It is worth learning the most common of these by heart.

Singular	Plural
aoibhinn *pleasant*	**aoibhne**
bodhar *deaf*	**bodhra**
daingean *solid*	**daingne**
deacair *difficult*	**deacra**
domhain *deep*	**doimhne**
folamh *empty*	**folmha**
íseal *low*	**ísle**
láidir *strong*	**láidre**
milis *sweet*	**milse**
ramhar *fat*	**ramhra**
saibhir *rich*	**saibhre**
sleamhain *slippery*	**sleamhna**
socair *quiet*	**socra**
uasal *noble*	**uaisle**

- Note that the adjective is not usually aspirated in the plural.

  an bhean <u>bh</u>eag   *the wee woman*

  na mná <u>b</u>eaga   *the wee women*

- If the adjective comes after a noun that ends in a **slender consonant** in the plural, i.e. if the final consonant is preceded by **i**, it must be aspirated.

  an fear <u>mór</u>   *the big man*

  na fir m<u>h</u>óra   *the big men*

1.4 Singular adjectives in the dative case

- The way the noun changes in the dative case affects what happens to the attributive adjective that goes with it.

⇨ See section 3.2 of chapter 2 on the use of nouns in the dative case.

- If the noun is eclipsed in the dative case the adjective takes the common form shown above.

an fear mór	*the big man*
leis an bhfear mór	*with the big man*
an bhean mhór	*the big woman*
leis an mbean mhór	*with the big woman*

- If the noun is aspirated in the dative case the adjective is also aspirated.

an fear mór	*the big man*
leis an fhear mhór	*with the big man*
an bhean mhór	*the big woman*
leis an bhean mhór	*with the big woman*

1.5 Plural attributive adjectives in the dative case

Plural adjectives in the dative case are the same as the common form plural shown above.

na fir mhóra	*the big men*
leis na fir mhóra	*with the big men*
na fuinneoga beaga	*the little windows*
ar na fuinneoga beaga	*on the little windows*

1.6 Singular attributive adjectives in the vocative case

> ### Típ
> Remember, the vocative case is used when addressing someone.

- Adjectives in the vocative case are aspirated.

  a dhuine chóir   *dear man*

  a phobal dhil   *faithful community*

- The ending of the adjective isn't usually changed in the vocative case.

  a Liam bheag   *wee Liam*

  a Bhrónach dhil   *faithful Brónach*

- The endings of **Group 1 nouns** are changed in the vocative case and when this happens an **i** is inserted into the ending of some adjectives ending in a broad consonant.

  a fhir mhóir   *big man*

  a Sheáin bhig   *little Seán*

⇨ See section 2.1 of chapter 2 on Nouns for information on Group 1 nouns.

> ### Típ
> This insertion of an **i** before the final consonant also happens to some adjectives in the genitive singular. For more information see below.

1.7 Plural adjectives in the vocative case

- Plural adjectives are not aspirated in the vocative case.

a dhaoine maithe	*good people*
a fheara móra	*great men*

- The endings of the plural adjectives take the same form in the vocative case as they do in the common form plural as shown above.

na fir mhaithe	*the good men*
a fheara maithe	*good men*
na mná beaga	*the small women*
a mhná beaga	*small women*

1.8 Singular attributive adjectives in the genitive case

The beginning and the ending of singular adjectives in the genitive case depend on whether the noun they describe is masculine or feminine.

➤**Masculine nouns**

- An adjective describing a masculine noun is aspirated in the genitive case when possible

an fear mór	*the big man*
hata an fhir mhóir	*the hat of the big man*
an carr gasta	*the fast car*
doras an chairr ghasta	*the door of the fast car*

- If the adjective ends with a consonant preceded by *a, á, o, ó, u* or *ú*, an *i* is usually added to the genitive case ending.

an carr dubh	*the black car*
doras an chairr dhuibh	*the door of the black car*
an rang mór	*the big class*
daltaí an ranga mhóir	*the students of the big class*

- If the adjective ends with a consonant preceded by *e, é, i* or *í*, no change is usually made to the genitive case ending.

an teach maith	*the good house*
díon an tí mhaith	*the roof of the good house*
an gasúr cáiliúil	*the famous boy*
ainm an ghasúir cháiliúil	*the name of the famous boy*

- If the adjective ends in *-ach* or *-each* the ending changes to *-aigh* or *-igh* in the genitive case.

an teach salach	*the dirty house*
díon an tí shalaigh	*the roof of the dirty house*
an fear tuirseach	*the tired man*
méanfach an fhir thuirsigh	*the yawn of the tired man*

- If the adjective ends in a vowel the ending does not change in the genitive case.

an fear cróga	*the brave man*
máthair an fhir chróga	*the mother of the brave man*
an rang fada	*the long class*
ábhar an ranga fhada	*the subject of the long class*

Típ

When used with masculine nouns, the ending of some adjectives does not change in the genitive case. These can be broken up into three groups.

1. Some adjectives with one syllable ending in **-ch** or **-cht**, for example:

    caoch (blind), **fliuch** (wet), **lách** (friendly), **moch** (early), **nocht** (naked)

2. Some adjectives with one syllable ending in a double consonant, for example:

    mall (slow), **corr** (strange), **cearr** (wrong), **gearr** (short), **teann** (tight)

3. The following adjectives:

    cúng (narrow), **deas** (nice), **mear** (fast), **searbh** (bitter), **tiubh** (thick), **trom** (heavy), **tur** (dry)

➤Feminine nouns

- An adjective describing a feminine noun is not aspirated in the genitive case.

an bhean bheag	the wee woman
hata na mná bige	the wee woman's hat
an bhróg mhór	the big shoe
iall na bróige móire	the lace of the big shoe

- If the adjective ends in a **slender consonant** an **-e** is added to the end in the genitive case.

an ghirseach chiúin	*the quiet girl*
béal na girsí ciúine	*the mouth of the quiet girl*
an bhean mhaith	*the good woman*
teach na mná maithe	*the house of the good woman*

- If the adjective ends in a **broad consonant** an *i* is usually added before the consonant, which is then followed by **-e**.

an bhróg mhór	*the big shoe*
iall na bróige móire	*the lace of the big shoe*
an oíche fhuar	*the cold night*
teocht na hoíche fuaire	*the temperature of the cold night*

- When there is a pair of vowels in the middle of an adjective a change takes place:

éa → éi

an scian ghéar	*the sharp knife*
cos na scine géire	*the handle of the sharp knife*

ea → ei

an bhróg dheas	*the nice shoe*
iall na bróige deise	*the lace of the nice shoe*

ea → i

an bhean bheag	*the small woman*
teach na mná bige	*the house of the small woman*

ia → éi

an bhróg liath	the grey shoe
iall na bróige léithe	the lace of the grey shoe

ío → í

an ghrian fhíor	the true sun
solas na gréine fíre	the light of the true sun

io → i

an bhean fhionn	the blonde woman
gruaig na mná finne	the hair of the blonde woman

iu → i

an oíche fhliuch	the wet night
lár na hoíche fliche	the middle of the wet night

- If the adjective ends in **-úil** it changes to **-úla** in the genitive case.

an bhean cáiliúil	the famous woman
guth na mná cáiliúla	the famous woman's voice
an ghirseach spéisiúil	the interesting girl
caint na girsí spéisiúla	the interesting girl's talk

- If the adjective ends in **-ach** or **-each** it changes to **-aí** or **-í** in the genitive case.

an chos shalach	the dirty foot
ionga na coise salaí	the nail of the dirty foot
an lann dhíreach	the straight blade
cos na lainne dírí	the handle of the straight blade

- If the adjective ends in a vowel it is not changed in the genitive case.

an bhean chalma	*the calm woman*
guth na mná calma	*the voice of the calm women*
an ghirseach chróga	*the brave girl*
máthair na girsí cróga	*the mother of the brave girl*

- The adjectives **cóir** (*just*), **deacair** (*difficult*) and **socair** (*quiet*) are changed to **córa**, **deacra** and **socra** in the genitive case.

1.9 Plural attributive adjectives in the genitive case

- An adjective added to a plural noun is never aspirated or eclipsed in the genitive case.

na fir bheaga	*the wee men*
teach na bhfear beag	*the house of the wee men*
na hócáidí móra	*the big occasions*
láthair na n-ócáidí móra	*the venue of the big occasions*

- The ending of an adjective added to a plural noun in the genitive case depends on how the genitive plural of the noun is formed.

- If a noun's genitive plural ending is the same as that of its common form singular, the adjective also takes the common form singular ending.

an gasúr maith	*the good boy*
máithreacha na ngasúr maith	*the mothers of the good boys*

an bhróg dheas	*the nice shoe*
stíl na mbróg deas	*the style of the nice shoes*

- If a noun's genitive plural ending is the same as that of its common form plural, the adjective also takes the common form plural ending.

na daoine suimiúla	*the interesting people*
rang na ndaoine suimiúla	*the class of the interesting people*
na háiteanna suimiúla	*the interesting places*
muintir na n-áiteanna suimiúla	*the people of the interesting places.*

➪ See section 4 of chapter 2 on Nouns for more information on the ending of nouns in the genitive.

2 Degrees of comparison of adjectives

What are degrees of comparison?
Degrees of comparison are used when we compare one person
or one thing with another using the comparative or superlative.
Another degree of comparison is that of equality.

2.1 The degree of equality

- The degree of equality concerns the similarity between two
  people or things. In Irish we use ***chomh ... le ...*** to translate
  as ... as... in English.

  Tá Máire <u>chomh</u> hóg <u>le</u> Seán.   *Mary is as young as Seán.*

  Tá mise <u>chomh</u> mór <u>leatsa</u>.   *I'm as big as you.*

- Notice that ***chomh*** or ***le*** don't aspirate but they add an **h-** before
  vowels.

2.2 The comparative

- The comparative is used when we compare two nouns or
  pronouns. In Irish, the word ***níos*** and a special form of the
  adjective are used for this.

  Tá sé níos fuaire inniu.   *It is colder today.*

- ***ná*** can be placed after the adjective and this is the same as *than*
  in English.

  Tá Seán <u>níos airde ná Pól</u>.   *Seán is taller than Pól.*

  Tá buachaillí <u>níos spórtúla</u>   *Boys are more sporty than girls.*
  <u>ná cailíní</u>.

2.3 The superlative

- The superlative is used to emphasize one extreme of a group.
  In Irish, the word **is** and a special form of the adjective are used
  for this.

  Is é an múinteoir _is fearr_ é.   *He is the best teacher.*

  Is é Seán an duine _is airde_   *Seán is the tallest person in the class.*
  sa rang.

2.4 Forming the comparative and superlative

- The forms of the adjective used for the comparative and the
  superlative are the same.

- This form is the same as the form that is used in the genitive
  singular feminine of adjectives as shown above.

- If the adjective ends with a slender consonant the comparative
  and the superlative forms are usually formed by adding **-e** to the
  end.

  Tá an cailín ciú_in_.   *The girl is quiet.*

  Tá an cailín eile níos ciú_ine_ *The other girl is quieter than her.*
  ná í.

  Tá Máire a_it_.   *Mary is strange.*

  Is í Síle an cailín is a_ite_.   *Síle is the strangest girl.*

- If the adjective ends in a broad consonant the comparative and
  superlative forms are usually formed by adding **i** before the
  consonant and **-e** after it.

  Tá an lá inniu fu_ar_.   *Today is cold.*

Beidh an lá amárach níos fua_ire_.	*Tomorrow will be colder.*
Tá Seán _ard_.	*Seán is tall.*
Is é Pól an duine is a_irde_.	*Pól is the tallest person.*

i When there is a pair of vowels in the middle of the adjective, the same changes take place as are listed on page 40.

- If the adjective ends in **-úil** the ending is changed to **-úla** to form the comparative and the superlative.

Tá an bhean sin cáili_úil_.	*That woman is famous.*
Tá an bhean eile níos cáili_úla_.	*The other woman is more famous.*
Tá an ghirseach sin spéisi_úil_.	*That girl is interesting.*
Is í an ghirseach eile an duine is spéisi_úla_.	*The other girl is the most interesting person.*

- If the adjective ends in **-ach** or **-each** this changes to **-aí** or **-í** in the comparative and the superlative.

Tá an chos chlé sal_ach_.	*The left foot is dirty.*
Tá an chos dheas níos sal_aí_.	*The right foot is dirtier.*
Tá an líne sin dír_each_.	*That line is straight.*
Is í an líne eile an ceann is dír_í_.	*The other line is the straightest one.*

- If the adjective ends in a vowel there is no change in the comparative and the superlative.

Tá Máire calm_a_.	*Mary is calm.*
Tá Síle níos calm_a_.	*Síle is calmer.*

| **Tá Seán ru<u>a</u>.** | *Seán is red-haired.* |
| **Is é Pól an duine is ru<u>a</u>.** | *Paul is the most red-haired.* |

- If the adjective ends in **-air** this changes to **-cra** in the comparative and the superlative.

Tá an cheist seo deac<u>air</u>.	*This question is difficult.*
Tá an cheist eile níos deac<u>ra</u>.	*The other question is more difficult.*
Tá an Seán soc<u>air</u>.	*Seán is quiet.*
Is é Pól an duine is soc<u>ra</u>.	*Pól is the quietest person.*

[i] There are some adjectives that have irregular comparative and superlative forms. It is worth learning the most common of these by heart.

Basic form	Comparative	Superlative
beag *small*	**níos lú** *smaller*	**is lú** *smallest*
breá *fine*	**níos breátha** *finer*	**is breátha** *finest*
dócha *probable*	**níos dóichí** *more probable*	**is dóichí** *most probable*
fada *far*	**níos faide** *further*	**is faide** *furthest*
furasta *easy*	**níos fusa** *easier*	**is fusa** *easiest*
ionúin *beloved*	**níos ansa** *more beloved*	**is ansa** *most beloved*
maith *good*	**níos fearr** *better*	**is fearr** *best*
mór *big*	**níos mó** *bigger*	**is mó** *biggest*

olc bad	*níos measa* worse	*is measa* worst
te warm	*níos teo* warmer	*is teo* warmest

3 The verbal adjective

> **What is a verbal adjective?**
> A verbal adjective is made from a verb. It can be used either as a
> normal adjective or as a verb with the help of an auxiliary verb.

3.1 The verbal adjective as a normal adjective

- The verbal adjective can be used both as an attributive adjective
  and as a predicative adjective. Look at these sentences:

  I. **Is bean <u>phósta</u> í.**   *She is a married woman.*
  II. **Tá an bhean <u>pósta</u> anois.**   *The woman is married now.*

- In the first sentence, the verbal adjective (**phósta**) is linked
  directly to the noun (**bean**), so it is acting as an attributive
  adjective.

- In the second sentence, the verbal adjective (**pósta**) is linked
  indirectly to the noun (**bhean**) using a linking verb (**tá**).

- When acting like an adjective the verbal adjective is subject to
  the same rules as described above for other normal adjectives.

3.2 The verbal adjective used with an auxiliary verb

- The verbal adjective can be used with an auxiliary verb to
  describe a verbal action in the perfect tense. Look at these
  English sentences:

  I. *They have finished.*
  II. *He had left.*

- To express this tense in Irish the auxiliary verb **bí** is used with the verbal adjective.

  I. *Tá siad críochnaithe.*
  II. *Bhí sé imithe.*

- Now look at these English sentences:

  III. *Seán has eaten the bread.*
  IV. *Pól had done the work.*

- To translate these structures in Irish, the auxiliary verb **bí** is used with the verbal adjective and the preposition **ag**.

  III. *Tá an t-arán ite ag Seán.*
  IV. *Bhí an obair déanta ag Pól.*

3.3 Forming the verbal adjective

- The verbal adjective is formed from the base form of the verb. The most common way of forming the verbal adjective is by adding *-ta, -te, -tha* or *-the*. Sometimes *-fa, -a* or *-e* is added, but these aren't as common.

- We can split verbs into three groups as regards the endings added to them to form their verbal adjective.

➤**Group 1: -ta, -te**

- We usually add *-ta* or *-te* to verbs whose base forms end with *-d, -n, -l, -s* or *-ch*. *-ta* is added to base forms with a broad ending and *-te* is added to base forms with a slender ending.

Ending in -d

Broad	Slender
coimhéad guard → *coimhéadta*	*úsáid* use → *úsáidte*
stad stop → *stadta*	*creid* believe → *creidte*

Ending in -n

Broad	Slender
déan do → *déanta*	*seinn* play → *seinnte*
dún close → *dúnta*	*bain* cut → *bainte*

Ending in -l

Broad	Slender
díol sell → *díolta*	*buail* hit → *buailte*
triall test → *triallta*	*mill* spoil → *millte*

Ending in -s

Broad	Slender
seas stand → *seasta*	*bris* break → *briste*
leigheas cure → *leigheasta*	*gluais* move → *gluaiste*

Ending in -ch

Broad	Slender
tóch dig → *tóchta*	*sroich* reach → *sroichte*
croch hang → *crochta*	----------------------

- If the base form of the verb ends in **-th**, we lose these letters and add **-te**.

Broad	Slender
-----------------------	**caith** throw → **cai<u>te</u>**
-----------------------	**ith** eat → **i<u>te</u>**

- If it is a verb with a short base form (one syllable) ending in **-gh**, we lose these letters and add **-te**.

Broad	Slender
-----------------------	**léigh** read → **léi<u>te</u>**
-----------------------	**luaigh** mention → **luai<u>te</u>**

➤ **Group 2: -tha, -the**

- We usually add these endings to verbs whose base forms end with **-b, -c, -g, -m, -p** or **-r. -tha** is added to base forms with a broad ending and **-the** is added to base forms with a slender ending.

Ending in -b

Broad	Slender
scuab brush → **scuab<u>tha</u>**	-----------------------
lúb bend → **lúb<u>tha</u>**	-----------------------

Ending in -c

Broad	Slender
pléasc explode → **pléasc<u>tha</u>**	**coisc** ban → **coisc<u>the</u>**

nasc *join* → **nasctha**	**stróic** *tear* → **stróicthe**

Ending in -g

Broad	Slender
leag *knock down* → **leagtha**	**lig** *let* → **ligthe**
fág *leave* → **fágtha**	**tuig** *understand* → **tuigthe**

Ending in -m

Broad	Slender
cum *make up* → **cumtha**	**foghlaim** *learn* → **foghlamtha**
cam *bend* → **camtha**	**creim** *erode* → **creimthe**

[i] Some stems, like **foghlaim**, lose the **i** before the final consonant when forming the verbal adjective. Since this **i** has been lost, it takes the ending **-tha** because the stem now ends in a broad consonant. Another example is:

> **díolaim** *collect* → **díolamtha**

Ending in -p

Broad	Slender
ceap *appoint* → **ceaptha**	**scaip** *spread* → **scaipthe**
crap *contract* → **craptha**	**teip** *fail* → **teipthe**

Ending in -r

Broad	Slender
gearr cut → **gearrtha**	**cuir** put → **curtha**
cíor brush → **cíortha**	**fair** watch → **fairthe**

ⓘ Some base forms, like **cuir**, lose the *i* before the final consonant when forming the verbal adjective. Since this *i* has been lost, it takes the ending **-tha** because the stem now ends in a broad consonant. Another example is:

buair worry → **buartha**

- If a verb with a long base form (two syllables) ends in **-aigh** or **-igh** we lose the **-gh** and add **-the**.

Broad	Slender
ceannaigh buy → **ceannaithe**	**éirigh** get up → **éirithe**
clúdaigh cover → **clúdaithe**	**imigh** leave → **imithe**

- If the base form of the verb ends in **-bh** or **-mh** and is broad we lose these letters and add **-fa**.

Broad	Slender
gabh go → **gafa**	----------------------
scríobh write → **scríofa**	----------------------

- If the base form of the verb ends in **-t** we add **-a** or **-e** to the end. **-a** is added to base forms with a broad ending and **-e** is added to stems with a slender ending.

Broad	Slender
cleacht practise → **cleacht_a_**	**loit** spoil → **loit_e_**
at swell → **at_a_**	**suigh** sit → **suit_e_**

i It is worth learning the verbal adjective forms for the irregular verbs by heart.

Base form	Verbal adjective
abair say	**ráite**
beir bear	**beirthe**
bí be	**bheith**
clois hear	**cloiste**
déan do	**déanta**
faigh get	**faighte**
feic see	**feicthe**
ite eat	**ite**
tabhair get	**tugtha**
tar come	**tagtha**
téigh go	**dulta**

4 Possessive adjectives

What is a possessive adjective?
A possessive adjective is an adjective used with a noun to show ownership or possession.

- The possessive adjectives in Irish are **mo, do, a** (masculine), **a** (feminine), **ár, bhur, a** (plural). These correspond to the English possessive adjectives *my, your, his, her, our, your, their*.

- The possessive adjective may change the noun that follows it. The changes caused are as follows:

➤ **mo, do, a** (masculine)

- These adjectives aspirate nouns beginning with a consonant, if possible.

mo theach	*my house*
do bhróg	*your shoe*
a charr	*his car*

- If the noun begins with a vowel **mo** and **do** change to **m'** and **d'**; **a** does not change. No change is made to the noun.

m'athair	*my father*
d'ordóg	*your thumb*
a aintín	*his aunt*

➤*a* (feminine)

- This adjective causes no change to nouns beginning with a consonant.

a teach	*her house*
a bróg	*her shoe*
a carr	*her car*

- If the noun begins with a vowel an *h* is added before it.

a hathair	*her father*
a hordóg	*her thumb*
a haintín	*her aunt*

➤*ár, bhur, a*

- These adjectives eclipse nouns beginning with a consonant, if possible.

ár gcarranna	*our cars*
bhur ngaolt a	*your relations*
a bpócaí	*their pockets*

- If the noun begins with a vowel an *n-* is added before it.

ár n-athair	*our father*
bhur n-oidí	*your tutors*
a n-iníonacha	*their daughters*

KEY POINTS

✔ Adjectives in Irish can be either attributive or predicative.
✔ Attributive adjectives must agree with the noun they are describing in number and in case.
✔ Adjectives which are formed from verbs are known as verbal adjectives.

VERBS

What is a verb?
A **verb** is a 'doing' word which describes what someone or something does, what someone or something is, or what happens to them, for example, *run, cry, jump*.

1 Overview of verbs

- Unlike in English, the verb comes first in the sentence in Irish, with the person, place or thing carrying out the action of the verb following it.

- The base form of the verb is the one found in the dictionary. In Irish this form is also used as the **Imperative** to give orders and instructions. **Ól** (meaning *to drink*), for example, is also the form we use to tell someone to drink something.

- All forms of regular verbs, in all tenses, are formed from the base form of the verb.

- There are 11 irregular verbs in Irish which do not follow the same pattern as the other verbs.

- The **tense** of a verb indicates the time at which the action took place. In Irish, there is the **present** (*I run*), the **past** (*I ran*) and the **future** (*I will run*).
  The **conditional mood** can refer to the **past**, **present** or **future** (*I would run/I would have run*).

- Sometimes in Irish we have **synthetic** verb forms. This means that the verb, person and tense are expressed as one word: *ithim* (*I eat*).

KEY POINTS

✔ Irish verbs come at the beginning of the sentence and are followed by a noun or a pronoun.
✔ The imperative of the verb and the base form of the verb are the same in Irish.
✔ Sometimes the pronoun, when it is functioning as the subject of the verb, can be incorporated into the form of the verb, making one word.
✔ There are 11 irregular verbs in Irish.

2 Categorizing verbs

As mentioned above, verbs in Irish are categorized by their base form, which is the form shown in the dictionary. They belong to the **first conjugation** (broad or slender), the **second conjugation** (broad or slender), or are irregular.

2.1 The first conjugation

- Single-syllable verbs, like **bris** (*break*), **mol** (*praise*) and **luigh** (*lie*), and verbs of more than one syllable which end in **-áil** and **-áin**, like **sábháil** (*save*), belong to this conjugation.

- The verb is known as **broad** if the last vowel is **a, o,** or **ú**. The verb is known as **slender** if the last vowel is **i**, except in the case of verbs ending in **-áil** and **-áin**, which are **broad**.

Broad	Slender
amharc look	**bris** break
can sing	**buail** hit
fág leave	**caill** lose
fás grow	**caith** wear/throw/spend/ smoke
féach look	**creid** believe
íoc pay	**éist** listen
ól drink	**fill** return
tóg lift	**goid** steal
sábháil save	**lig** let
marcáil mark	**tuig** understand
taispeáin show	**úsáid** use

2.2 The second conjugation

- Most verbs of more than one syllable belong to this conjugation. Most of these verbs end in **-igh**, like **deisigh** (*repair*). Some end in **-il, -ir** and **-is**, like **ceangail** (*tie*), **imir** (*play*) and **inis** (*tell*).

- The verb is known as **broad** if it ends in **-aigh**, and **slender** if it ends in **-igh**. If it ends in **-ail**, it is **broad**, and if it ends in **-il, -ir** and **-is**, it is **slender**.

Broad	Slender
ardaigh *raise*	**aimsigh** *locate*
athraigh *change*	**ceistigh** *question*
brostaigh *rush*	**coinnigh** *keep*
cabhraigh *help*	**deisigh** *repair*
ceannaigh *buy*	**dírigh** *straighten*
diúltaigh *refuse*	**éirigh** *get up*
éalaigh *escape*	**imigh** *leave*
mothaigh *feel*	**sínigh** *sign*
tosaigh *begin*	**imir** *play*
ceangail *tie*	**inis** *tell*

3 The imperative

> **What is the imperative?**
> The **imperative** is the form of the verb used to tell someone to do
> something. The base form of the verb is used for this.

Dún an doras!	*Shut the door!*
Tóg an leabhar!	*Pick up the book!*
Éist leis an cheol!	*Listen to the music!*
Cuir an ar an tábla.	*Put the pen on the table.*
Sábháil an madra!	*Save the dog!*
Taispeáin dom an pictiúr.	*Show me the picture.*

3.1 Forming the imperative

i If we want to tell more than one person to do something,
we must add an ending to the base form of the verb. The ending
we add depends on the conjugation of the verb, or the spelling of
its base form.

➤**First conjugation verbs**

- If the last vowel of the verb is **broad** (*a, o* or *ú*), we add *-aigí*:

   Dúnaigí an doras!   *Shut the door!*
   (said to more than one person)

   Tógaigí na leabhair!   *Pick up the books!*
   (said to more than one person)

- If the last vowel of the verb is **slender** (**i**), we add **-igí**:

  Éistigí leis an múinteoir!   *Listen to the teacher, children!*

  Cuirigí bhur lámha in airde!   *Put your hands up, boys!*

- If the verb ends in **-áil** or **-áin**, we remove the letter **i** before adding the ending:

  sábháil (*save*) → **sábhál<u>aigí</u>**

  Sábhálaigí bhur gcuid airgid,   *Save your money, my friends!*
  a chaired!

  taispeáin (*show*) → **taispeán<u>aigí</u>**

  Taispeánaigí dom bhur gcuid   *Show me your work, girls!*
  oibre, a chailíní!

- With verbs such as **téigh** (*heat*) or **dóigh** (*burn*), we must remove the **-igh** before adding **-igí** to the ending:

  téigh (*heat*) → **té<u>igí</u>**

  Téigi bhur dtithe le   *Heat your houses with electricity!*
  leictreachas!

  dóigh (*burn*) → **dó<u>igí</u>**

  Dóigí an bruscar seo, a fheara!   *Burn this rubbish, men!*

Broad	Slender
amharcaigí *look*	**brisigí** *break*
canaigí *sing*	**buailigí** *hit*
fágaigí *leave*	**cailligí** *lose*

fásaigí *grow*	**caithigí** *wear/throw/spend/smoke*
féachaigí *look*	**creidigí** *believe*
íocaigí *pay*	**éistigí** *listen*
ólaigí *drink*	**filligí** *return*
tógaigí *lift*	**goidigí** *steal*
sábhálaigí *save*	**ligigí** *let*
marcálaigí *mark*	**tuigigí** *understand*
taispeánaigí *show*	**úsáidigí** *use*

➤ **Second conjugation verbs**

- If the verb ends in **-igh**, we change the **-igh** to **-ígí**:

    ceannaigh (*buy*) → **ceannaígí**

    Ceannaígí milseáin, a thaiscí!   *Buy sweets, my dears!*

    éirigh (*get up*) → **éirígí**

    Eirígí go luath amárach,   *Get up early tomorrow, children!*
    a pháistí!

- If the verb has more than one syllable and is broad (ends in **-ail, -ain** or **-ais**), we remove the **-ai** and add **-aígí**:

    ceangail (*tie*) → **ceanglaígí**

    Ceanglaígí bhur mbróga   *Tie your shoes properly, boys!*
    mar is ceart, a bhuachaillí!

oscail (open) → **osclaígí**

**Osclaígí bhur leabhair,   *Open your books, girls!*
a chailíní!**

- If the verb has more than one syllable and is slender (ends in **-il,
-in** or **-is**), we remove the **-i** and add **-ígí**:

imir (play) → **imrígí**

Imrígí go deas, a pháistí!   *Play nicely, children!*

inis (tell) → **insígí**

Insígí an fhírinne, a thaiscí!   *Tell me the truth, dears!*

Broad	Slender
ardaigí raise	**aimsígí** locate
athraígí change	**ceistígí** question
brostaígí rush	**coinnígí** keep
cabhraígí help	**deisígí** repair
ceannaígí buy	**dírígí** straighten
diúltaígí refuse	**éirígí** get up
éalaígí escape	**imígí** leave
mothaígí feel	**sínígí** sign
tosaígí begin	**imrígí** play
ceanglaígí tie	**insígí** tell

3.2 The negative of the imperative

- To tell someone not to do something all we have to do is to put
ná before the imperative, whether it is singular or plural.

***Ná** caith an liathróid, a Mhicheáil.*	*Don't throw the football, Michael!*
***Ná** caithigí brúscar, a pháistí.*	*Don't throw rubbish, children!*

- If the verb begins with a vowel, we must place ***h*** at the beginning of this verb after the negative ***ná***.

Ná hól an t-uisce sin!	*Don't drink the water!*
Ná himrígí peil ar an mbóthar!	*Don't play football on the road!*

3.3 Irregular verbs

There are 11 **irregular verbs** in Irish. These are verbs that don't follow the same patterns as the other verbs.

Base form/imperative	Plural imperative
bí *be*	***bígigí***
tar *come*	***tagaigí***
téigh *go*	***téigí***
feic *see*	***feicigí***
cluin/clois *hear*	***cluinigí/cloisigí***
abair *say*	***abraigí***
déan *do/make*	***déanaigí***
beir *grab*	***beirigí***
faigh *get*	***faighigí***
tabhair *give*	***tugaigí***
ith *eat*	***ithigí***

4   The past tense

> **What is the past tense?**
> The **past tense** in Irish is the verb tense we use to talk about
> completed actions in the past, for example, *I ran home yesterday*.

4.1   Forming the past tense

►There are four main ways in which we change the base form of the
verb in Irish in order to form the past tense:

1. **Aspirate** the initial letter of the verb.
2. Make **no change** to the initial letter of the verb.
3. Place *d'* in front of the initial letter of the verb.
4. Place *d'* in front of the initial letter of the verb, and also **aspirate**.

►We then simply add the **subject** of the verb – the person or thing
carrying out the action in the verb. In Irish, these are:

mé	*I*
tú	*you* (singular)
sé	*he*
sí	*she*
amar[1]/eamar[2]/aíomar[3]/íomar[4] or **muid**	*we**
sibh	*you* (plural)
siad	*they*

[1] First Conjugation Broad – we add these forms to the end of the verb
[2] First Conjugation Slender – we add these forms to the end of the verb
[3] Second Conjugation Broad – we add these forms to the end of the verb
[4] Second Conjugation Slender – we add these forms to the end of the verb

* The form of '*we*' which we choose depends on the whether the verb is first

or second conjugation. If we use **muid** we don't need to worry about the conjugation used. **Muid** is usually used in Ulster Irish.

►**Aspiration:** If the base form of the verb begins with the letters **b, c, d, g, m, p, s, t**, we aspirate to form the past tense.

Base form	Past tense
bris *break*	**Bhris mé na rialacha.** *I broke the rules.*
can *sing*	**Chan sé an t-amhrán.** *He sang the song.*
dún *close*	**Dhún sí an doras.** *She closed the door.*
goid *steal*	**Ghoid an gasúr an t-airgead.** *The boy stole the money.*
mol *praise*	**Mhol sé an gasúr.** *He praised the boy.*
póg *kiss*	**Phóg sé an cailín.** *He kissed the girl.*
siúil *walk*	**Shiúil mé abhaile.** *I walked home.*
tóg *lift*	**Thóg mé an leabhar.** *I picked up the book.*

►**No change:** There are certain letters and combinations of letters at the beginning of verbs which cannot be aspirated in the past tense. These are **l, n, r, sc, sm, sp, st**.

Base form	Past tense
las *light*	**Las mé an tine.** *I lit the fire.*
nigh *wash*	**Nigh mé mo lámha.** *I washed my hands.*
rith *run*	**Rith siad abhaile.** *They ran home.*
scríobh *write*	**Scríobh sí litir.** *She wrote a letter.*
smaoinigh *think*	**Smaoiníomar ar an lá.** *We thought about the day.*
spreag *inspire*	**Spreag an scannán mé.** *The film inspired me.*
stad *stop*	**Stad siad láithreach.** *They stopped straight away.*

➤ If the stem of the verb begins with a **vowel** (*a/á, e/é, i/í, o/ó, u/ú*), we place *d'* in front of the verb:

Base form	Past tense
amharc watch	**D'amharc mé.** *I watched.*
éist listen	**D'éist siad.** *They listened.*
ith eat	**D'itheamar an dinnéar.** *We ate the dinner.*
ól drink	**D'ól tú cupán tae.** *You drank a cup of tea.*
ullmhaigh prepare	**D'ullmhaigh sí an dinnéar.** *She prepared the dinner.*

➤ If the stem of the verb begins with the letter *f*, we both aspirate and place *d'* in front of the verb:

Base form	Past tense
fan wait	<u>**D'fh**</u>**an mé.** *I waited.*
fág leave	<u>**D'fh**</u>**ág siad.** *They left.*
fill return	<u>**D'fh**</u>**illeamar.** *We returned.*

4.2 Asking and answering questions with verbs in the past tense

➤ To ask questions in the past tense, we put *ar* before the past tense verb:

Bhris sé an fhuinneog.   *He broke the window.*

Ar bhris sé an fhuinneog?   *Did he break the window?*

➤If the verb has a *d'* in front of it in the past tense, we drop the *d'* when asking questions:

D'ól sí barraíocht. *She drank too much.*

Ar ól sí barraíocht? *Did she drink too much?*

➤To form the negative in the past tense, we put **níor** before the past tense verb:

Bhris sé an fhuinneog. *He broke the window.*

Níor bhris sé an fhuinneog. *He didn't break the window.*

➤If the verb has a *d'* in front of it in the past tense, we drop the *d'* when answering in the negative:

D'ól sé. *(Yes,) he drank.*

Níor ól sé. *(No,) he didn't drink*

Típ

There are no words for *Yes* and *No* in Irish. Instead, we answer by using the verb in the question. In English, this would be the same as saying:

Question: *Did you eat your breakfast?*
Answer: *I ate/I did not eat.*

4.3 Irregular verbs in the past tense

➤Some irregular verbs change considerably in the past tense, becoming very unlike the base form of the verb. Luckily there are only 11 of them!

	Past tense	Negative	Question
bí be	**bhí mé** I was	**ní raibh mé**	**an raibh mé**
	bhí tú you were	**ní raibh tú**	**an raibh tú**
	bhí sé he was	**ní raibh sé**	**an raibh sé**
	bhí sí she was	**ní raibh sí**	**an raibh sí**
	bhíomar/bhí muid we were	**ní rabhamar/ raibh muid**	**an rabhamar/ raibh muid**
	bhí sibh you (plural) were	**ní raibh sibh**	**an raibh sibh**
	bhí siad they were	**ní raibh siad**	**an raibh siad**
tar come	**tháinig mé** I came	**níor tháinig mé**	**ar tháinig mé**
	tháinig tú you came	**níor tháinig tú**	**ar tháinig tú**
	tháinig sé he came	**níor tháinig sé**	**ar tháinig sé**
	tháinig sí she came	**níor tháinig sí**	**ar tháinig sí**
	thángamar/ tháinig muid we came	**níor thángamar/ tháinig muid**	**ar thángamar/ tháinig muid**
	tháinig sibh you (plural) came	**níor tháinig sibh**	**ar tháinig sibh**
	tháinig siad they came	**níor tháinig siad**	**ar tháinig siad**

	Past tense	Negative	Question
téigh *go*	**chuaigh mé** *I went*	*ní dheachaigh mé*	*an ndeachaigh mé*
	chuaigh tú *you went*	*ní dheachaigh tú*	*an ndeachaigh tú*
	chuaigh sé *he went*	*ní dheachaigh sé*	*an ndeachaigh sé*
	chuaigh sí *she went*	*ní dheachaigh sí*	*an ndeachaigh sí*
	chuamar/ **chuaigh muid** *we went*	*ní dheachamar/* *ní dheachaigh* *muid*	*an ndeachamar/* *an ndeachaigh* *muid*
	chuaigh sibh *you (plural) went*	*ní dheachaigh* *sibh*	*an ndeachaigh* *sibh*
	chuaigh siad *they went*	*ní dheachaigh* *siad*	*an ndeachaigh* *siad*
feic *see*	**chonaic mé** *I saw*	*ní fhaca mé*	*an bhfaca mé*
	chonaic tú *you saw*	*ní fhaca tú*	*an bhfaca tú*
	chonaic sé *he saw*	*ní fhaca sé*	*an bhfaca sé*
	chonaic sí *she saw*	*ní fhaca sí*	*an bhfaca sí*
	chonaiceamar/ **chonaic muid** *we saw*	*ní fhacamar/* *fhaca sibh*	*an bhfacamar/* *bhfaca muid*
	chonaic sibh *you (plural) saw*	*ní fhaca sibh*	*an bhfaca sibh*
	chonaic siad *they saw*	*ní fhaca siad*	*an bhfaca siad*

	Past tense	Negative	Question
clois hear	**chuala mé** I heard	**níor chuala mé**	**ar chuala mé**
	chuala tú you heard	**níor chuala tú**	**ar chuala tú**
	chuala sé he heard	**níor chuala sé**	**ar chuala sé**
	chuala sí she heard	**níor chuala sí**	**ar chuala sí**
	chualamar/ **chuala muid** we heard	**níor chualamar/** **chuala muid**	**ar chualamar/** **chuala muid**
	chuala sibh you (plural) heard	**níor chuala sibh**	**ar chuala sibh**
	chuala siad they heard	**níor chuala siad**	**ar chuala siad**
abair say	**dúirt mé** I said	**ní dúirt mé**	**an ndúirt mé**
	dúirt tú you said	**ní dúirt tú**	**an ndúirt tú**
	dúirt sé he said	**ní dúirt sé**	**an ndúirt sé**
	dúirt sí she said	**ní dúirt sí**	**an ndúirt sí**
	dúramar/dúirt **muid** we said	**ní dúramar/** **dúirt muid**	**an ndúramar/** **ndúirt muid**
	dúirt sibh you (plural) said	**ní dúirt sibh**	**an ndúirt sibh**
	dúirt siad they said	**ní dúirt siad**	**an ndúirt siad**

	Past tense	Negative	Question
déan do/ make	**rinne mé** I did/made	**ní dhearna mé**	**an ndearna mé**
	rinne tú you did/made	**ní dhearna tú**	**an ndearna tú**
	rinne sé he did/made	**ní dhearna sé**	**an ndearna sé**
	rinne sí she did/made	**ní dhearna sí**	**an ndearna sí**
	rinneamar/ rinne muid we did/made	**ní dhearnamar/ dhearna muid**	**an ndearnamar/ ndearna muid**
	rinne sibh you (plural) did/ made	**ní dhearna sibh**	**an ndearna sibh**
	rinne siad they did/made	**ní dhearna siad**	**an ndearna siad**
beir grab	**rug mé** I grabbed	**níor rug mé**	**ar rug mé**
	rug tú you grabbed	**níor rug tú**	**ar rug tú**
	rug sé he grabbed	**níor rug sé**	**ar rug sé**
	rug sí she grabbed	**níor rug sí**	**ar rug sí**
	rugamar we grabbed	**níor rugamar/ rug muid**	**ar rugamar/ rug muid**
	rug sibh you (plural) grabbed	**níor rug sibh**	**ar rug sibh**
	rug siad they grabbed	**níor rug siad**	**ar rug siad**

	Past tense	Negative	Question
faigh *get*	**fuair mé** *I got*	*ní bhfuair mé*	*an bhfuair mé*
	fuair tú *you got*	*ní bhfuair tú*	*an bhfuair tú*
	fuair sé *he got*	*ní bhfuair sé*	*an bhfuair sé*
	fuair sí *she got*	*ní bhfuair sí*	*an bhfuair sí*
	fuaireamar *we got*	*ní bhfuaramar/ bhfuair muid*	*an bhfuaramar/ bhfuair muid*
	fuair sibh *you (plural) got*	*ní bhfuair sibh*	*an bhfuair sibh*
	fuair siad *they got*	*ní bhfuair siad*	*an bhfuair siad*
tabhair *give*	**thug mé** *I gave*	*níor thug mé*	*ar thug mé*
	thug tú *you gave*	*níor thug tú*	*ar thug tú*
	thug sé *he gave*	*níor thug sé*	*ar thug sé*
	thug sí *she gave*	*níor thug sí*	*ar thug sí*
	thugamar *we gave*	*níor thugamar/ thug muid*	*ar thugamar/ thug muid*
	thug sibh *you (plural) gave*	*níor thug sibh*	*ar thug sibh*
	thug siad *they gave*	*níor thug siad*	*ar thug siad*

	Past tense	Negative	Question
	d'ith mé *I ate*	*níor ith mé*	*ar ith mé*
	d'ith tú *you ate*	*níor ith tú*	*ar ith tú*
	d'ith sé *he ate*	*níor ith sé*	*ar ith sé*
ith *eat*	*d'ith sí* *she ate*	*níor ith sí*	*ar ith sí*
	d'itheamar *we ate*	*níor itheamar/ ith muid*	*ar itheamar/ ith muid*
	d'ith sibh *you (plural) ate*	*níor ith sibh*	*ar ith sibh*
	d'ith siad *they ate*	*níor ith siad*	*ar ith siad*

5 The present tense

What is the present tense?
In English the **present tense** is used to talk about what is true
at the moment, what happens regularly, and what is happening
now.

5.1 The present habitual tense

- The present habitual tense in Irish refers to activities that
  happen on a **regular** basis. It does not refer to what is
  happening right now. We will deal with this in a later
  section.

- Like the other tenses, the present habitual tense is formed from
  the base form of the verb. We add an ending to the base form,
  and then the subject of the verb, if it is a pronoun:

  Bris Break   **Bris_eann_ tú** You break

- When deciding what ending to add to the verb, it is important
  to know whether the verb is first conjugation broad or slender,
  or second conjugation broad or slender.

➤**First conjugation verbs**

- If the last vowel of the verb is **broad** (*a, o* or *ú*), we add:

aim	I
ann tú	you
ann sé	he
ann sí	she
aimid	we
ann sibh	you (plural)
ann siad	they

Dún*aim* an doras má chluinim an clog. I open the door if I hear the bell.

Scríobh*ann* sí litir uair sa mhí. She writes a letter once a month.

Ól*aimid* tae go minic. We drink tea often.

- If the last vowel of the verb is **slender** (*i*), we add:

im	I
eann tú	you
eann sé	he
eann sí	she
imid	we
eann sibh	you (plural)
eann siad	they

Éist*im* gach lá. I listen every day.

Bris*eann* siad na rialacha gach lá. They break the rules every day.

- If the verb ends in **-áil** or **-áin**, we remove the letter **i** before adding the **broad** endings:

aim	I
ann tú	you
ann sé	he
ann sí	she
aimid	we
ann sibh	you (plural)
ann siad	they

Taispeán<u>aimid</u> an scannán go minic.   *We often show the film.*

➤ **Second conjugation verbs**

- If the verb ends in **-aigh**, we remove the **-aigh** and add the following endings:

aím	I
aíonn tú	you
aíonn sé	he
aíonn sí	she
aímid	we
aíonn sibh	you (plural)
aíonn siad	they

Ceann<u>aím</u> bia gach lá.   *I buy food every day.*

Brost<u>aíonn</u> siad abhaile gach oíche.   *They hurry home every evening.*

- If the verb ends in **-igh**, we remove the **-igh** and add the following endings:

ím	I
íonn tú	you
íonn sé	he
íonn sí	she
ímid	we
íonn sibh	you (plural)
íonn siad	they

Éir<u>ím</u> go luath ar maidin.   *I get up early in the morning.*

Oibr<u>íonn</u> sí go dian.   *She works hard.*

- If the verb has more than one syllable and is broad (ends in **-ail, -ain** or **-ais**), we remove the **-ai** and add the **broad** endings:

aím	I
aíonn tú	you
aíonn sé	he
aíonn sí	she
aímid	we
aíonn sibh	you (plural)
aíonn siad	they

Ceangl<u>aíonn</u> sí a bróga gach maidin.   *She ties her shoes every morning.*

Oscl<u>aímid</u> na fuinneoga gach tráthnóna.   *We open the windows every afternoon.*

- If the verb has more than one syllable and is slender (ends in
  -il, -in or **-is**), we remove the **-i** and add the **slender** endings:

ím	*I*
íonn tú	*you*
íonn sé	*he*
íonn sí	*she*
ímid	*we*
íonn sibh	*you* (plural)
íonn siad	*they*

> **Imr<u>ím</u> peil le mo chara.**   *I play football with my friend.*
>
> **Ins<u>íonn</u> sí an scéal sin gach lá.**   *She tells that story every day.*

5.2 Asking and answering questions with verbs in the present tense

➤ To ask questions in the present tense, we put **an** before the present
tense verb, and **eclipse** the first letter of the verb. This means that
we place a letter in front of the initial letter of the verb. Verbs
beginning with vowels **are not** eclipsed:

> **briseann sé** *he breaks*   **an mbriseann sé?** *does he break?*
>
> **ólann siad** *they drink*   **an ólaimid?** *do we drink?*

➤ To answer in the negative in the present tense, we put **ní** before
the present tense verb, and **aspirate** the first letter of the verb.
This means we place the letter **h** after the first letter of the verb.
Ní does nothing to words beginning with vowels:

> **Ólann siad.**   *They drink.*
>
> **An ólann siad?**   *Do they drink?*
>
> **Ní ólann siad.**   *(No,) they don't drink.*

5.3 Irregular verbs in the present tense

Some irregular verbs change in the present tense.

	Present habitual	Negative	Question
bí *be*	**bím** *I am*	**ní bhím**	**an mbím**
	bíonn tú *you are*	**ní bhíonn tú**	**an mbíonn tú**
	bíonn sé *he is*	**ní bíonn sé**	**an mbíonn sé**
	bíonn sí *she is*	**ní bhíonn sí**	**an mbíonn sí**
	bímid *we are*	**ní bhímid**	**an mbímid**
	bíonn sibh *you* (plural) *are*	**ní bhíonn sibh**	**an mbíonn sibh**
	bíonn siad *they are*	**ní bhíonn siad**	**an mbíonn siad**
tar *come*	**tagaim** *I come*	**ní thagaim**	**an dtagaim**
	tagann tú *you come*	**ní thagann tú**	**an dtagann tú**
	tagann sé *he comes*	**ní thagann sé**	**an dtagann sé**
	tagann sí *she comes*	**ní thagann sí**	**an dtagann sí**
	tagaimid *we come*	**ní thagaimid**	**an dtagaimid**
	tagann sibh *you* (plural) *come*	**ní thagann sibh**	**an dtagann sibh**
	tagann siad *they come*	**ní thagann siad**	**an dtagann siad**

	Present habitual	Negative	Question
téigh *go*	**téim** *I go*	*ní théim*	*an dtéim*
	téann tú *you go*	*ní théann tú*	*an dtéann tú*
	téann sé *he goes*	*ní théann sé*	*an dtéann sé*
	téann sí *she goes*	*ní théann sí*	*an dtéann sí*
	téimid *we go*	*ní théimid*	*an dtéimid*
	téann sibh *you (plural) go*	*ní théann sibh*	*an dtéann sibh*
	téann siad *they go*	*ní théann siad*	*an dtéann siad*
feic *see*	**feicim** *I see*	*ní fheicim*	*an bhfeicim*
	feiceann tú *you see*	*ní fheiceann tú*	*an bhfeiceann tú*
	feiceann sé *he sees*	*ní fheiceann sé*	*an bhfeiceann sé*
	feiceann sí *she sees*	*ní fheiceann sí*	*an bhfeiceann sí*
	feicimid *we see*	*ní fheicimid*	*an bhfeicimid*
	feiceann sibh *you (plural) see*	*ní fheiceann sibh*	*an bhfeiceann sibh*
	feiceann siad *they see*	*ní fheiceann siad*	*an bhfeiceann siad*

	Present habitual	Negative	Question
clois hear	cloisim I hear	ní chloisim	an gcloisim
	cloiseann tú you hear	ní chloiseann tú	an gcloiseann tú
	cloiseann sé he hears	ní chloiseann sé	an gcloiseann sé
	cloiseann sí she hears	ní chloiseann sí	an gcloiseann sí
	cloisimid we hear	ní chloisimid	an gcloisimid
	cloiseann sibh you (plural) hear	ní chloiseann sibh	an gcloiseann sibh
	cloiseann siad they hear	ní chloiseann siad	an gcloiseann siad
abair say	deirim I say	ní deirim	an ndeirim
	deir tú you say	ní deir tú	an ndeir tú
	deir sé he says	ní deir sé	an ndeir sé
	deir sí she says	ní deir sí	an ndeir sí
	deirimid we say	ní deirimid	an ndeirimid
	deir sibh you (plural) say	ní deir sibh	an ndeir sibh
	deir siad they say	ní deir siad	an ndeir siad

	Present habitual	Negative	Question
dean *do/* *make*	**déanaim** *I do/make*	*ní dhéanaim*	*an ndéanaim*
	déanann tú *you do/make*	*ní dhéanann tú*	*an ndéanann tú*
	déanann sé *he does/makes*	*ní dhéanann sé*	*an ndéanann sé*
	déanann sí *she does/makes*	*ní dhéanann sí*	*an ndéanann sí*
	déanaimid *we do/make*	*ní dhéanaimid*	*an ndéanaimid*
	déanann sibh *you (plural) do/* *make*	*ní dhéanann sibh*	*an ndéanann sibh*
	déanann siad *they do/make*	*ní dhéanann siad*	*an ndéanann siad*
beir *grab*	**beirim** *I grab*	*ní bheirim*	*an mbeirim*
	beireann tú *you grab*	*ní bheireann tú*	*an mbeireann tú*
	beireann sé *he grabs*	*ní bheireann sé*	*an mbeireann sé*
	beireann sí *she grabs*	*ní bheireann sí*	*an mbeireann sí*
	beirimid *we grab*	*ní bheirimid*	*an mbeirimid*
	beireann sibh *you (plural) grab*	*ní bheireann sibh*	*an mbeireann sibh*
	beireann siad *they grab*	*ní bheireann siad*	*an mbeireann siad*

	Present habitual	Negative	Question
faigh get	faighim I get	ní fhaighim	an bhfaighim
	faigheann tú you get	ní fhaigheann tú	an bhfaigheann tú
	faigheann sé he gets	ní fhaigheann sé	an bhfaigheann sé
	faigheann sí she gets	ní fhaigheann sí	an bhfaigheann sí
	faighimid we get	ní fhaighimid	an bhfaighimid
	faigheann sibh you (plural) get	ní fhaigheann sibh	an bhfaigheann sibh
	faigheann siad they get	ní fhaigheann siad	an bhfaigheann siad
tabhair give	tugaim I give	ní thugaim	an dtugaim
	tugann tú you give	ní thugann tú	an dtugann tú
	tugann sé he gives	ní thugann sé	an dtugann sé
	tugann sí she gives	ní thugann sí	an dtugann sí
	tugaimid we give	ní thugaimid	an dtugaimid
	tugann sibh you (plural) give	ní thugann sibh	an dtugann sibh
	tugann siad they give	ní thugann siad	an dtugann siad

	Present habitual	Negative	Question
ith eat	ithim I eat	ní ithim	an ithim
	itheann tú you eat	ní itheann tú	an itheann tú
	itheann sé he eats	ní itheann sé	an itheann sé
	itheann sí she eats	ní itheann sí	an itheann sí
	ithimid we eat	ní ithimid	an ithimid
	itheann sibh you (plural) eat	ní itheann sibh	an itheann sibh
	itheann siad they eat	ní itheann siad	an itheann siad

6 The future tense

> **What is the future tense?**
> The **future tense** is the verb tense used to talk about something
> that will happen or will be true.

6.1 Forming the future tense

- Like the other tenses, the future tense is formed from the base
  form of the verb. In this tense, as in the present tense, we add
  the ending to the base form before we add the subject of the
  verb, if it is a pronoun.

- When deciding what ending to add to the verb, it is important
  to know whether the verb is first conjugation broad or slender,
  or second conjugation broad or slender.

⇨ See section 2 on page 65.

- **First conjugation verbs**

- If the last vowel of the verb is **broad** (*a, o* or *ú*), we add:

faidh mé	I
faidh tú	you
faidh sé	he
faidh sí	she
faimid	we
faidh sibh	you (plural)
faidh siad	they

Dúnfaidh *mé an doras.*	*I will open the door.*
Scríobhfaidh *sí litir.*	*She will write a letter.*
Ófaimid *tae.*	*We will drink tea.*

- If the last vowel of the verb is **slender** (*i*), we add:

fidh mé	I
fidh tú	you
fidh sé	he
fidh sí	she
fimid	we
fidh sibh	you (plural)
fidh siad	they

Éistfidh *mé gach lá.*	*I will listen every day.*
Brisfidh *siad na rialacha gach lá.*	*They will break the rules every day.*

- If the verb ends in **-áil** or **-áin**, we remove the letter **i** before adding the **broad** endings:

faidh mé	I
faidh tú	you
faidh sé	he
faidh sí	she
faimid	we
faidh sibh	you (plural)
faidh siad	they

Taispeánfaimid *an scannán go minic.*	*We will often show the film.*

➤Second conjugation verbs

- If the verb ends in **-aigh**, we remove the **-aigh** and add the following **broad** endings:

óidh mé	I
óidh tú	you
óidh sé	he
óidh sí	she
óimid	we
óidh sibh	you (plural)
óidh siad	they

Ceannóidh mé bia gach lá. — I will buy food every day.

Brostóidh siad abhaile gach oíche. — They will hurry home every evening.

- If the verb ends in **-igh**, we remove the **-igh** and add the following **slender** endings:

eoidh mé	I
eoidh tú	you
eoidh sé	he
eoidh sí	she
eoidh	we
eoidh sibh	you (plural)
eoidh siad	they

Éireoidh mé go luath ar maidin. — I will get up early in the morning.

Oibreoidh sí go dian. — She will work hard.

- If the verb has more than one syllable and is broad (ends in *-ail*, *-ain* or *-ais*), we remove the *-ai* and add the **broad** endings:

óidh mé	I
óidh tú	you
óidh sé	he
óidh sí	she
óimid	we
óidh sibh	you (plural)
óidh siad	they

Ceanglóidh sí a bróga gach maidin. *She will tie her shoes every morning.*

Osclóimid na fuinneoga gach tráthnóna. *We will open the windows every afternoon.*

- If the verb has more than one syllable and is slender (ends in *-il*, *-in* or *-is*), we remove the *-i* and add the **slender** endings:

eoidh mé	I
eoidh tú	you
eoidh sé	he
eoidh sí	she
eoidh	we
eoidh sibh	you (plural)
eoidh siad	they

Imreoidh mé peil le mo chara. *I will play football with my friend.*

Inseoidh sí an scéal sin gach lá. *She will tell that story every day.*

6.2 Asking and answering questions

➤To ask questions in the future tense, we put **an** before the future tense verb, and eclipse the first letter of the verb. Verbs beginning with vowels **are not** eclipsed:

brisfidh sé	*he will break*	**an mbrisfidh sé?**	*will he break?*
ólfaidh siad	*they will drink*	**an ólfaidh siad?**	*will they drink?*

➤To answer in the negative in the future tense, we put **ní** before the future tense verb, and aspirate the first letter of the verb. **ní** does nothing to words beginning with vowels:

Ní bhrisfidh mé na rialacha.	*I will not break the rules.*
Ní ólfaidh mé ag deoch sin.	*I will not drink that drink.*

6.3 Irregular verbs in the future tense

Some irregular verbs change in the future tense.

	Present habitual	Negative	Question
	beidh mé *I will be*	**ní bheidh mé**	**an bheidh mé**
	beidh tú *you will be*	**ní bheidh tú**	**an bheidh tú**
	beidh sé *he will be*	**ní bheidh sé**	**an bheidh sé**
bí *be*	**beidh sí** *she will be*	**ní bheidh sí**	**an bheidh sí**
	beimid *we will be*	**ní bheimid**	**an bheimid**
	beidh sibh *you (plural) will be*	**ní bheidh sibh**	**an bheidh sibh**
	beidh siad *they will be*	**ní bheidh siad**	**an bheidh siad**

	Present habitual	Negative	Question
tar come	**tiocfaidh mé** I will come	ní thiocfaidh mé	an thiocfaidh mé
	tiocfaidh tú you will come	ní thiocfaidh tú	an thiocfaidh tú
	tiocfaidh sé he will come	ní thiocfaidh sé	an thiocfaidh sé
	tiocfaidh sí she will come	ní thiocfaidh sí	an thiocfaidh sí
	tiocfaimid we will come	ní thiocfaimid	an thiocfaimid
	tiocfaidh sibh you (plural) will come	ní thiocfaidh sibh	an thiocfaidh sibh
	tiocfaidh siad they will come	ní thiocfaidh siad	an thiocfaidh siad
téigh go	**rachaidh mé** I will go	ní rachaidh mé	an rachaidh mé
	rachaidh tú you will go	ní rachaidh tú	an rachaidh tú
	rachaidh sé he will go	ní rachaidh sé	an rachaidh sé
	rachaidh sí she will do	ní rachaidh sí	an rachaidh sí
	rachaimid we will go	ní rachaimid	an rachaimid
	rachaidh sibh you (plural) will go	ní rachaidh sibh	an rachaidh sibh
	rachaidh siad they will go	ní rachaidh siad	an rachaidh siad

	Present habitual	Negative	Question
feic *see*	**feicfidh mé** *I will see*	*ní fheicfidh mé*	*an fheicfidh mé*
	feicfidh tú *you will see*	*ní fheicfidh tú*	*an fheicfidh tú*
	feicfidh sé *he will see*	*ní fheicfidh sé*	*an fheicfidh sé*
	feicfidh sí *she will see*	*ní fheicfidh sí*	*an fheicfidh sí*
	feicfimid *we will see*	*ní fheicfimid*	*an fheicfimid*
	feicfidh sibh *you (plural) will see*	*ní fheicfidh sibh*	*an fheicfidh sibh*
	feicfidh siad *they will see*	*ní fheicfidh siad*	*an fheicfidh siad*
clois *hear*	**cloisfidh mé** *I will hear*	*ní chloisfidh mé*	*an chloisfidh mé*
	cloisfidh tú *you will hear*	*ní chloisfidh tú*	*an chloisfidh tú*
	cloisfidh sé *he will hear*	*ní chloisfidh sé*	*an chloisfidh sé*
	cloisfidh sí *she will hear*	*ní chloisfidh sí*	*an chloisfidh sí*
	cloisfimid *we will hear*	*ní chloisfimid*	*an chloisfimid*
	cloisfidh sibh *you (plural) will hear*	*ní chloisfidh sibh*	*an chloisfidh sibh*
	cloisfidh siad *they will hear*	*ní chloisfidh siad*	*an chloisfidh siad*

	Present habitual	Negative	Question
abair say	*déarfaidh mé* I will say	*ní déarfaidh mé*	*an déarfaidh mé*
	déarfaidh tú you will say	*ní déarfaidh tú*	*an déarfaidh tú*
	déarfaidh sé he will say	*ní déarfaidh sé*	*an déarfaidh sé*
	déarfaidh sí she will say	*ní déarfaidh sí*	*an déarfaidh sí*
	déarfaimid we will say	*ní déarfaimid*	*an déarfaimid*
	déarfaidh sibh you (plural) will say	*ní déarfaidh* *sibh*	*an déarfaidh* *sibh*
	déarfaidh siad they will say	*ní déarfaidh*	*an déarfaidh*
déan do/ make	*déanfaidh mé* I will do/make	*ní dhéanfaidh* *mé*	*an ndéanfaidh* *mé*
	déanfaidh tú you will do/make	*ní dhéanfaidh tú*	*an ndéanfaidh* *tú*
	déanfaidh sé he will do/make	*ní dhéanfaidh sé*	*an ndéanfaidh* *sé*
	déanfaidh sí she will do/make	*ní dhéanfaidh sí*	*an ndéanfaidh sí*
	déanfaimid we will do/make	*ní dhéanfaimid*	*an ndéanfaimid*
	déanfaidh sibh you (plural) will do/ make	*ní dhéanfaidh* *sibh*	*an ndéanfaidh* *sibh*
	déanfaidh siad they will do/make	*ní dhéanfaidh* *siad*	*an ndéanfaidh* *siad*

	Present habitual	Negative	Question
beir grab	**béarfaidh mé** I will grab	ní bhéarfaidh mé	an mbéarfaidh mé
	béarfaidh tú you will grab	ní bhéarfaidh tú	an mbéarfaidh tú
	béarfaidh sé he will grab	ní bhéarfaidh sé	an mbéarfaidh sé
	béarfaidh sí she will grab	ní bhéarfaidh sí	an mbéarfaidh sí
	béarfaimid we will grab	ní bhéarfaimid	an mbéarfaimid
	béarfaidh sibh you (plural) will grab	ní bhéarfaidh sibh	an mbéarfaidh sibh
	béarfaidh siad they will grab	ní bhéarfaidh siad	an mbéarfaidh siad
faigh get	**gheobhaidh mé** I will get	ní bhfaighidh mé	an bhfaighidh mé
	gheobhaidh tú you will get	ní bhfaighidh tú	an bhfaighidh tú
	gheobhaidh sé he will get	ní bhfaighidh sé	an bhfaighidh sé
	gheobhaidh sí she will get	ní bhfaighidh sí	an bhfaighidh sí
	gheobhaimid we will get	ní bhfaighimid	an bhfaighimid
	gheobhaidh sibh you (plural) will get	ní bhfaighidh sibh	an bhfaighidh sibh
	gheobhaidh siad they will get	ní bhfaighidh siad	an bhfaighidh siad

	Present habitual	Negative	Question
tabhair give	**tabharfaidh mé** I will give	**ní thabharfaidh mé**	**an dtabharfaidh mé**
	tabharfaidh tú you will give	**ní thabharfaidh tú**	**an dtabharfaidh tú**
	tabharfaidh sé he will give	**ní thabharfaidh sé**	**an dtabharfaidh sé**
	tabharfaidh sí she will give	**ní thabharfaidh sí**	**an dtabharfaidh sí**
	tabharfaimid we will give	**ní thabharfaimid**	**an dtabharfaimid**
	tabharfaidh sibh you (plural) will give	**ní thabharfaidh sibh**	**an dtabharfaidh sibh**
	tabharfaidh siad they will give	**ní thabharfaidh siad**	**an dtabharfaidh siad**
ith eat	**íosfaidh mé** I will eat	**ní íosfaidh mé**	**an íosfaidh mé**
	íosfaidh tú you will eat	**ní íosfaidh tú**	**an íosfaidh tú**
	íosfaidh sé he will eat	**ní íosfaidh sé**	**an íosfaidh sé**
	íosfaidh sí she will eat	**ní íosfaidh sí**	**an íosfaidh sí**
	íosfaimid we will eat	**ní íosfaimid**	**an íosfaimid**
	íosfaidh sibh you (plural) will eat	**ní íosfaidh sibh**	**an íosfaidh sibh**
	íosfaidh siad they will eat	**ní íosfaidh siad**	**an íosfaidh siad**

THE VERB 'TO BE' IN THE PRESENT TENSE

An unusual aspect of the verb *to be* in Irish is that it has two forms in the present tense, a **habitual present**, which is used for events that happen regularly, and an **immediate present**, which is used for events that are occurring at the present time.

Look at the difference in between the following sentences:

a. ***Bíonn sé fuar in Éirinn sa gheimhreadh.***   *It is cold in Ireland in the winter.*

b. ***Tá sé fuar in Éirinn inniu.***   *It is cold in Ireland today.*

Sentence 'a' states how the weather <u>usually</u> is, whilst sentence 'b' states how the weather <u>actually</u> is at the present moment.

1   The habitual present tense of the verb 'to be'

Positive	Negative	Question
bím *I am*	**ní bhím**	**an mbím**
bíonn tú *you are*	**ní bhíonn tú**	**an mbíonn tú**
bíonn sé *he is*	**ní bhíonn sé**	**an mbíonn sé**
bíonn sí *she is*	**ní bhíonn sí**	**an mbíonn sí**
bímid *we are*	**ní bhímid**	**an mbímid**
bíonn sibh *you (plural) are*	**ní bhíonn sibh**	**an mbíonn sibh**
bíonn siad *they are*	**ní bhíonn siad**	**an mbíonn siad**

Bím sa teach sin gach seachtain.	I am in that house every week.
Bíonn sé anseo gach oíche Luain.	He is here every Monday night.
Ní bhíonn sí ar scoil go minic.	She is not often at school.
An mbíonn tú breoite go minic?	Are you often ill?
Ní bhíonn siad in Éirinn in am ar bith.	They are never in Ireland.

In all these examples, these are regular events.

2 The immediate present tense of the verb 'to be'

Positive	Negative	Question
tá mé/táim I am	**níl mé/nílim**	**an bhfuil mé/ bhfuilim**
tá tú you are	**níl tú**	**an bhfuil tú**
tá sé he is	**níl sé**	**an bhfuil sé**
tá sí she is	**níl sí**	**an bhfuil sí**
táimid we are	**nílimid**	**an bhfuilimd**
tá sibh you (plural) are	**níl sibh**	**an bhfuil sibh**
tá siad they are	**níl siad**	**an bhfuil siad**

Tá mé sa teach anois.	I am in the house now.
Tá sé anseo faoi láthair.	He is here at present.
Níl sí ar scoil ar maidin.	She is not at school this morning.
An bhfuil tú breoite inniu?	Are you ill today?
Níl siad in Éirinn an mhí seo.	They aren't in Ireland this month.

THE COPULA

What is the copula?

The **copula** *is* in Irish is a kind of grammatical equals sign. It is used to express what a person or a thing is (e.g. *John is a footballer*, *they are teachers*, *Mary is a young girl*). It is used in **classification** sentences (*he is a man*), **identification** sentences (*Carmel is the lawyer*), and **with the preposition** *le* to express **ownership**. The copula can be positive, negative or in question form, and can appear in the present or past tense.

Típ

When classifying nouns in Irish, some learners use *Tá mé* (*I am*) + noun. This cannot be done, and is a very common mistake. *Tá mé, tá tú* etc can only be followed by an adjective, an action or a preposition:

> *Tá mé ard.*   I am tall.
> *Tá tú ag obair.*   You are working.
> *Tá siad ar an urlár.*   They are on the floor.

1   Classification sentences

1.1   Overview

► These tell or ask what a person or thing is, or express a classification:

> **Is fear Colm.**   Colm is a man.
>
> **Is duine ard thú.**   You are a tall person.
>
> **Is polaiteoir cumasach é.** He is a competent politician.

Is leabhar maith é sin.   *That is a good book.*

Is cailín deas í.   *She is a nice girl.*

➤In classification sentences we always see the following:

- The subject: **Colm, thú, é, é sin** and **í** are the subjects in the examples above.

- The predicate: the information given about the subject: **fear, duine ard, polaiteoir cumasach, leabhar maith, cailín deas** are the predicates in the examples above.

- The copula: **is**, in the examples above.

➤The following is the normal word order of classification sentences:

Copula	Predicate	Subject	Meaning
Is	bean	í.	*She is a woman.*
Is	peileadóir	Liam.	*Liam is a footballer.*
Is	múinteoir maith	Tomás.	*Thomas is a good teacher.*
Is	gasúr cliste	thú.	*You are a clever boy.*
Is	dlúthchairde	iad.	*They are good friends.*
Is	duine deas	an príomhoide.	*The principal is a nice person.*

➤At times, although this is not necessary, a personal pronoun is placed in front of the subject if the subject is a definite noun:

Copula	Predicate	Subject	Meaning
Is	*cathair álainn*	<u>é</u> *An tIúr.*	*Newry is a beautiful town.*
Is	*ceoltóirí*	<u>ad</u> *Máire agus Dónal.*	*Máire and Dónal are musicians.*

Típ

If a noun is one of the following, it is known as a definite:

(i)   personal names/place names/names of countries/languages:

Máire

Seán

Gleann an Iolair   Glenullin

Béal Feirste   Belfast

An Fhrainc   France

An Iodáil   Italy

An Ghaeilge   Irish

An Spáinnis   Spanish

(ii) nouns after the article:

an teach   the house

na cailíní   the girls

(iii) nouns after possessive adjectives:

mo chara   my friend

do shláinte   your health

1.2 Interrogative pronouns in classification sentences

The interrogative pronouns **cad, cad é, céard** are used in the following classification sentences: **Cad seo? Cad é seo? Céard seo?** (What is this?); **Cad sin? Cad é sin? Céard é sin?** (What is that?). Their usage depends largely on dialect, with Ulster Irish favouring **cad é** and Munster and Connaught Irish favouring **cad/céard**.

Cad/cad é/céard é sin?	What is that?
Is gluaisteán mór é.	It is a big car.
Cad/cad é/céard é seo?	What is this?
Is nóta deich bpunt é.	It is a ten pound note.

1.3 The negative form in classification sentences

To form the negative, we change **is** to **ní**. Note that **ní** has no effect on the initial letter of the predicate in classification sentences.

Copula	Predicate	Subject	Meaning
Ní	fiaclóir	é.	He is not a dentist.
Ní	guthán maith	é sin.	That's not a good phone.
Ní	daoine deasa	Pól agus Síle.	Síle and Pól are not nice people.
Ní	bia sláintiúil	seacláid.	Chocolate is not a healthy food.
Ní	lá deas	é.	It is not a good day.
Ní	úll blasta	é.	It is not a tasty apple.

1.4 The question form in classification sentences

To form a question, we change **is** to **an**. Note that **an** has no effect on the initial letter of the predicate in classification sentences.

Copula	Predicate	Subject	Meaning
An	fiaclóir	é?	Is he a dentist?
An	guthán maith	é sin?	Is that a good phone?
An	daoine deasa	Pól agus Síle?	Are Síle and Pól nice people?
An	bia sláintiúil	seacláid?	Is chocolate a healthy food?
An	lá deas	é?	Is it a nice day?
An	úll blasta	é?	Is it a tasty apple?

1.5 The negative question form in classification sentences

To form a negative question, we change **is** to **nach**. Note that **nach** has no effect on the initial letter of the predicate in classification sentences.

Copula	Predicate	Subject	Meaning
Nach	seans iontach	é?	Isn't it a wonderful opportunity?
Nach	gasúr maith	thú?	Aren't you a good boy?
Nach	eitleán nua	é sin?	Isn't that a new plane?

Nach	scéalta suimiúla	iad?	Aren't they interesting stories?
Nach	clár leadránach	é?	Isn't it a boring programme?
Nach	cara maith	Micheál?	Isn't Micheál a good friend?

1.6 Reported speech in positive classification sentences

Reported speech is when we say something like "*I think [that] he is a nice boy*". In English, this is straightforward, but in Irish, the copula takes a special form and *is* changes to *gur*. *Gur* has no effect on the initial letter of the predicate in classification sentences.

Sílim... *I think...*

Copula	Predicate	Subject	Meaning
Gur	seans iontach	é.	I think [that] it is a wonderful opportunity.
Gur	gasúr maith	thú.	I think [that] you are a good boy.
Gur	eitleán nua	é sin.	I think [that] it is a new plane.
Gur	scéalta suimiúla	iad.	I think [that] they are interesting stories.
Gur	clár leadránach	é.	I think [that] it is a boring programme.

Gur	cara maith	Micheál.	I think [that] Micheál is a good friend.

1.7 Reported speech in negative classification sentences

For this we change the negative of the copula *ní* to **nach**. **Nach** has no effect on the initial letter of the predicate.

Deirtear... *It is said...*

Copula	Predicate	Subject	Meaning
Nach	rud cinnte	é.	*It is said [that] it is not a certainty.*
Nach	polaiteoir iontaofa	í.	*It is said [that] she is not a reliable politician.*

2   Identification sentences

2.1   Overview

➤When we tell or ask who a person or thing is or was we use an identification sentence:

Is mise an fear don phost.	*I am the man for the job.*
Is é Obama an tUachtarán.	*Obama is the President.*
Is í an bhean sin mo mháthair.	*That woman is my mother.*

➤In identification sentences we always see the following:

- The subject: ***an fear, an tUachtarán, mo mháthair*** are the subjects in the examples above. Note they are all definite nouns.

- The predicate: the information given about the subject: ***mise, Obama, an bhean sin***. Again, the predicate is always a definite noun, which serves to identify the subject as some particular person (***Peadar, Máire, Eoghan***), place (***An Fhrainc*** *France*, ***An Spáinn*** *Spain*, ***Meiriceá*** *America*) or a thing (***an tábla*** *the table*, ***an gluaisteán*** *the car*).

- The copula: **Is**, in the examples above.

[*i*]   When identifying, we sometimes use emphatic forms of the pronouns:

Pronoun	Emphatic form
mé	*mise*
thú	*thusa*
é	*eisean*
í	*ise*

sinn	sinne
sibh	sibhse
iad	iadsan

➤ The following is the normal word order of identification sentences:

Copula	Predicate	Subject	Meaning
Is	é Seán	an múinteoir.	Sean is the teacher.
Is	é An Dún	na buaiteoirí.	Down are the winners.
Is	iad na fir sin	na gadaithe.	Those men are the thieves.
Is	í Mairéad	an ceoltóir is fearr.	Mairéad is the best musician.
Is	tusa	an cara is fearr liom.	You are my best friend.

2.2 Interrogative pronouns in identification sentences

We normally use *cé* (who), followed by the appropriate pronoun:

Cé mé?	Who am I?
Cé thú?	Who are you?
Cé hé?	Who is he? (referring to a masculine noun)
Cé hé an múinteoir?	Who is the teacher?
Cé hí?	Who is she? (referring to a feminine noun)
Cé hí an bhanaisteoir?	Who is the actress?

Cé sinn?	Who are we?
Cé sibh?	Who are you? (plural)
Cé hiad?	Who are they?
Cé hiad na daoine sin?	Who are those people?

2.3 The negative form in identification sentences

To form the negative, we change *is* to *ní*. *Ní* prefixes the letter *h* to the pronouns *é, í* and *iad*:

Copula	Predicate	Subject	Meaning
Ní	<u>h</u>é Seán	an múinteoir.	Sean isn't the teacher.
Ní	<u>h</u>é An Dún	na buaiteoirí.	Down aren't the winners.
Ní	<u>h</u>iad na fir sin	na gadaithe.	Those men aren't the thieves.
Ní	<u>h</u>í Mairéad	an ceoltóir is fearr.	Mairéad isn't the best musician.
Ní	tusa	an cara is fearr liom.	You aren't my best friend.

2.4 The question form in identification sentences

To form the negative, we change *is* to *an*. Note that *an* has no effect on the initial letter of the predicate in identification sentences.

Copula	Predicate	Subject	Meaning
An	é Colm	an t-údar?	Is Colm the author?

An	í Áine	an bhanaltra?	Is Áine the nurse?
An	iad Seána agus Tarlach	na húinéirí?	Are Seána and Tarlach the owners?
An	sibhse	na hiomaitheoirí?	Are you the competitors?

2.5 The negative question form in identification sentences

To form the negative question, we change *is* to **nach**. Note that **nach** has no effect on the initial letter of the predicate in identification sentences.

Copula	Predicate	Subject	Meaning
Nach	é Colm	an t-údar?	Isn't Colm the author?
Nach	í Áine	an bhanaltra?	Isn't Áine the nurse?
Nach	iad Seána agus Tarlach	na húinéirí?	Aren't Seána and Tarlach the owners?
Nach	sibhse	na hiomaitheoirí?	Aren't you the competitors?

2.6 Reported speech in positive identification sentences

As in classification sentences, *is* changes to **gur**. If, however, the predicate has **é, í** or **iad** in front of it, it changes to **gurb**.

Sílim... *I think...*

Copula	Predicate	Subject	Meaning
Gur	*mise*	*an duine is fearr.*	I think that I am the best person.
Gurb	*é An Dún*	*na buaiteoirí.*	I think that Down are the winners.
Gurb	*iad na fir sin*	*na gadaithe.*	I think that those men are the thieves.
Gurb	*í Mairéad*	*an ceoltóir is fearr.*	I think that Mairéad is the best musician.
Gur	*tusa*	*an cara is fearr liom.*	I think that you are my best friend.

2.7 Reported speech in negative identification sentences

For this we change the negative of the copula **ní** to **nach**. **Nach** has no effect on the initial letter of the predicate.

Deirtear... *It is said...*

Copula	Predicate	Subject	Meaning
Nach	*é Cathal*	*an t-amhránaí.*	It is said that Cathal is not the singer.
Nach	*í Máirín*	*an bainisteoir.*	Is it said that Máirín isn't the manager.

3   The copula in the past tense

To use the copula in the past tense, we must change it slightly, but the sentence structure stays exactly the same as in the present tense. The copula in the past tense, however, can cause aspiration in some cases.

3.1   *Is*

Is changes to **ba** and aspirates the predicate. **Is** changes to **b'** if the predicate begins with a vowel. However, it stays as **ba** before the pronouns **é, í** and **iad** and cannot aspirate the other pronouns **mé, thú** etc.

➤**Classification sentences:**

Is ceoltóir Muiris.	*Muiris is a musician.*
Ba cheoltóir Muiris.	*Muiris was a musician.*
Is úll é sin.	*That is an apple.*
B'amhrán maith é sin.	*That was a good song.*

➤**Identification sentences:**

Is é Muiris an ceoltóir.	*Muiris is the musician.*
Ba é Muiris an ceoltóir.	*Muiris was the musician.*

3.2   *Ní*

Ní changes to **níor** and aspirates the predicate. **Is** does not change before vowels. **Níor** changes to **níorbh** before the pronouns **é, í** and **iad**.

➤**Classification sentences:**

Ní duine cliste é.	*He is not a clever person.*

Níor dhuine cliste é.	*He was not a clever person.*
Ní amharclann í.	*It is not a theatre.*
Níor amharclann í.	*It was not a theatre.*

➤ Identification sentences:

Ní hé Dónal mo chara.	*Dónal is not my friend.*
Níorbh é Dónal mo chara riamh.	*Dónal wasn't my friend.*

3.3 *An*

An changes to *ar* and aspirates the predicate. It does not change before vowels. **Ar** changes to **arbh** before the pronouns *é, í* and *iad*.

➤ Classification sentences:

An duine cliste é?	*Is he a clever person?*
Ar dhuine cliste é?	*Was he a clever person?*
An amharclann í?	*Is it a theatre?*
Ar amharclann í?	*Was it a theatre?*

➤ Identification sentences:

An é Dónal do chara?	*Is Dónal your friend?*
Arbh é Dónal do chara?	*Was Dónal your friend?*

3.4 *Nach*

Nach changes to *nár* and aspirates the predicate. It does not change before vowels. **Nár** changes to **nárbh** before the pronouns *é, í* and *iad*.

➤Identification sentences:

Nach teach mór é sin?	Isn't that a big house?
Nár t̲h̲each mór é sin?	Wasn't that a big house?
Nach aimsir ghalánta í?	Isn't it lovely weather?
Nár aimsir ghalánta í?	Wasn't it lovely weather?

➤Classification sentences:

Nach é an gasúr sin an freastalaí?	Isn't that boy the waiter?
Nárbh é an gasúr sin an freastalaí?	Wasn't that boy the waiter?

3.5 Gur

Gur stays the same but aspirates the predicate. It does not change before vowels. **Gurb** changes to **gurbh** before the pronouns **é, í** and **iad**.

➤Identification sentences:

Deir sé gur siopadóir é.	He says he is a shopkeeper.
Dúirt sé gur s̲h̲iopadóir é.	He says he was a shopkeeper.
Deir sé gur iománaí maith é.	He says he is a good hurler.
Dúirt sé gur iománaí maith é.	He says he was a good hurler.

➤Classification sentences:

Deir sé gurb é Seán an t-iománaí is fear.	He says Seán is the best hurler.
Dúirt sé gurbh é Seán an t-iománaí is fear.	He says Seán was the best hurler.

4 *Is* with the preposition *le* used to express ownership

4.1 Overview

➤ To express possession in Irish, we use a combination of **is** and the preposition **le**. The normal construction is:

Copula	+ Predicate	+ Subject	
Is	*le Liam*	*an gluaisteán*	*Liam owns the car.*

➤ When the predicate is someone's name, or a common noun, we place **le** in front of the name, and it causes no change, except to names which begin with vowels. In that case, we place **h** in front of the name:

Is le Michelle an rothar.	*Michelle owns the bike.*
Is le Ruairí an ticéad.	*Ruairí owns the ticket.*
Is le Malachaí é.	*Malachy owns it.*
Is le gasúr óg é.	*A young boy owns it.*
Is le hÚna an piano.	*Úna owns the piano.*

➤ When the predicate is preceded by the article **an** or **na**, **le** changes to **leis**. If the phrase is **leis an**, we either aspirate or eclipse the predicate. If the phrase is **leis na**, we do nothing to the predicate unless it begins with a vowel, in which case we place **h** at the beginning to the word. This is dealt with in the section on prepositions:

Is leis an fhear/bhfear é.	*The man owns it.*
Is leis na daoine sin iad.	*Those people own them.*
Is leis na hamhránaithe na cótaí sin.	*The singers own those coats.*

➤When the predicate is a pronoun, we use the following forms:

is liom *I own*

is leat *you own*

is leis *he owns*

is léi *she owns*   **+**   **Subject**

is linn *we own*

is libh *you own*

is leo *they own*

Típ
To ask who owns something, we say:

Cé leis é? (for masculine nouns) *Whose is it?/Who does it belong to?*

Cé leis í? (for feminine nouns) *Whose is it?/Who does it belong to?*

Cé leis iad? (for plural nouns) *Whose are they?/Who do they belong to?*

➤The past tense is formed by changing *is* to *ba*. No other changes are necessary.

4.2 The negative

➤The negative is formed by changing *is* to *ní*. *Ní* has no effect on the preposition *le* in any of its forms:

Ní le Séamus an teach sin.	*Séamus doesn't own that house.*
Ní liom an t-airgead seo.	*I don't own this money.*
Ní leis an bhean/mbean sin an leabhar.	*That woman doesn't own the book.*

➤ The past tense is formed by changing **ní** to **níor**. No other change is necessary.

4.3 Questions

➤ The question is formed by changing **is** to **an**. **An** has no effect on the preposition **le** in any of its forms:

An le Brónach an mála?	*Does Brónach own the bag?*
An leat an nuachtán sin?	*Do you own that newspaper?*
An leis an gharda/ngarda na heochracha?	*Does the guard own the keys?*

➤ The past tense is formed by changing **an** to **ar**. No other change is necessary.

➤ The negative question is formed by changing **is** to **nach**. **Nach** has no effect on the preposition **le** in any of its forms:

Nach leo na deochanna seo?	*Don't they own these drinks?*
Nach léi na bróga nua?	*Doesn't she own the new shoes?*
Nach leis an seanfhear an teach go fóill?	*Doesn't the old man still own the house?*

➤ The past tense is formed by changing **nach** to **nár**. No other change is necessary.

4.4 Reported speech

➤ Reported speech is formed by changing **is** to **gur**. **Gur** has no effect on the preposition **le** in any of its forms:

Deir sé gur liom é.	*He says I own it.*

Deir sé gur leis an fhoireann/   He says the team owns it.
   bhfoireann é.

➤There is no change necessary to **gur** in the past tense.

PARTICLES

What is a particle?
Verbal Particles in Irish come directly in front of the verb and can cause initial changes, such as aspiration and eclipsis, in the spelling of the verb.

1   Negative verbal particles

The negative verbal particles **ní/níor, cha/char** as well as the imperative **ná** change the meaning of the verb to *not* or *no*.

1.1   The negative particle *ní/níor*

Tense/ Mood	Particle	Aspirate or Eclipse	Example
Present	*ní*	Aspirate	**Ní bhrisfidh tú na rialacha arís.** *You will not break the rules again.*
Past	*níor*	Aspirate	**Níor cheannaigh mé nuachtán inniu.** *I didn't buy a newspaper today.*
Future	*ní*	Aspirate	**Ní sheasfaidh sé arís.** *It will not stand again.*
Conditional	*ní*	Aspirate	**Ní dhéanfainn a leithéid.** *I wouldn't do such a thing.*

Tense/Mood	Particle	Aspirate/Eclipse	Example
Past tense with 6 irregular verbs	*ní*	Aspirate/Eclipse	*ní raibh mé* *I was not* *ní dheachaigh mé* *I did not go* *ní dhearna mé* *I did not do/make* *ní bhfuair mé* *I did not get* *ní fhaca mé* *I did not see* *ní dúirt mé* *I did not say*

1.2 The imperative particle *ná*

Tense/Mood	Particle	Aspirate or Eclipse	Example
Imperative	*ná*	Prefixes *h* to verbs beginning with vowels	*Ná déan sin arís!* *Don't do that again!* *Ná hól an t-uisce sin!* *Don't drink that water!*

1.3 The interrogative particles *an/ar*

Tense/Mood	Particle	Aspirate or Eclipse	Example
Present	*an*	Eclipse. No effect on vowels	*An dtagann tú anseo go minic?* *Do you come here often?* *An itheann tú feoil?* *Do you eat meat?*

Past	*ar*	Aspirate. No effect on vowels	**Ar cheol sé an t-amhrán sin?** *Did he sing that song?* **Ar oscail tú an doras dó?** *Did you open the door for him?*
Future	*an*	Eclipse. No effect on vowels	**An ndéanfaidh tú gar dom?** *Will you do me a favour?* **An inseoidh tú an scéal dó?** *Will you tell him the story?*
Conditional	*an*	Eclipse. No effect on vowels	**An ndéarfadh sé sin dá mbeinnse anseo?** *Would he say that if I was here?* **An ullmhófá an dinnéar anocht dá mbeadh an t-am agat?** *Would you prepare the dinner tonight if you had the time?*
Past tense with 6 irregular verbs	*an*	Aspirate/ Eclipse	**An raibh tú ansin?** *Were you there?* **An ndeachaigh tú abhaile?** *Did you go home?* **An ndearna tú obair ar bith?** *Did you do any work?* **An bhfuair tú bronntanas deas?** *Did you get a nice present?* **An bhfaca tú an scannán?** *Did you see the film?* **An ndúirt tú rud ar bith leis?** *Did you say anything to him?*

1.4 The negative interrogative particles *nach/nár*

Tense/ Mood	Particle	Aspirate or Eclipse	Example
Present	*nach*	Eclipse. No effect on vowels	**An dtagann tú anseo go minic?** *Do you come here often?* **An itheann tú feoil?** *Do you eat meat?*
Past	*nár*	Aspirate. No effect on vowels	**Ar cheol sé an t-amhrán sin?** *Did he sing that song?* **Ar oscail tú an doras dó?** *Did you open the door for him*
Future	*nach*	Eclipse. No effect on vowels	**An ndéanfaidh tú gar dom?** *Will you do a favour for me?* **An inseoidh tú an scéal dó?** *Will you tell him the story?*
Conditional	*nach*	Eclipse. No effect on vowels	**An ndéarfadh sé sin dá mbeinnse anseo?** *Would he say that if I was here?* **An ullmhófá an dinnéar anocht?** *Would you prepare the dinner tonight?*

Past tense with 6 irregular verbs	*nach*	Aspirate/ Eclipse	**Nach raibh sé ann go luath?** *Was he not there early?* **Nach ndeachaigh siad ar saoire?** *Didn't they go on holiday?* **Nach ndearna sibh iarracht ar bith?** *Didn't you make any effort?* **Nach bhfuair tú airgead ar iasacht?** *Didn't you get a loan of money?* **Nach bhfaca sí an gluaisteán ag teacht?** *Didn't she see the car coming?* **Nach ndúirt siad sin cheana féin?** *Haven't they said that already?*

2 The relative particle

The relative particle is the word in Irish that translates English relative pronouns such as *that, who, whose* and *whom* in phrases like *the car that was damaged*; *the man whose car was damaged*.

⇨ For more on this see chapter 14 on Relative clauses.

2.1 The direct relative particle

Tense/ Mood	Particle	Aspirate or Eclipse	Example
Past	*a*	Aspirate	**Sin an fear a cheannaigh an teach?** *Is that the man who bought the house?*
Present	*a*	Aspirate	**Cá bhfuil an fear a bhíonn i mbun na hoibre de ghnáth?** *Where is the man who is usually in charge of the work?*
Future	*a*	Aspirate	**Is mise an bhean a dhéanfaidh an obair.** *I am the woman who will do the work.*
Conditional	*a*	Aspirate	**Sin duine a bheadh anseo dá mbeadh seans aige.** *There is a person who would be here if he had the chance.*

2.2 The indirect relative particle

Tense/ Mood	Particle	Aspirate or Eclipse	Example
Past	*ar*	Aspirate	*Sin an fear <u>ar</u> <u>ch</u>eannaigh mé teachuaidh.* That is the man <u>whom</u> I bought the house from.
Present	*a*	Eclipse. Prefixes *n-* to vowels	*Sin an poll <u>a</u> <u>d</u>tagann an luchóg amach as.* That's the hole <u>which</u> the mouse comes out of.
Future	*a*	Eclipse. Prefixes *n-* to vowels	*Sin an duine a mbeidh a mhac ag imirt anocht.* That's the person whose son will be playing tonight.
Conditional	*a*	Eclipse. Prefixes *n-* to vowels	*Sin duine a gceannóinn deoch dó.* That is a person <u>whom</u> I would buy a drink for.

3 *go/gur, sula, mura* *that, before, if not*

3.1 *go*

In reported statements in English the conjunction *that* can be left out: we can say *She says she's coming*, or *She says that she's coming*. In Irish, however, either **gur** or **go**, the words meaning *that*, must always be used.

Tense/ Mood	Particle	Aspirate or Eclipse	Example
Past	*gur*	Aspirate	***Dúirt sé gur cheannaigh sé teach nua.*** *He said that has bought a new house.*
Present	*go*	Eclipse. Prefixes *n-* to vowels	***Sílim go mbíonn sé anseo gach maidin.*** *I think that he is here every morning.* ***Sílim gon-ólann sé barraíocht.*** *I think that he drinks too much.*
Future	*go*	Eclipse. Prefixes *n-* to vowels	***Sílim go ndéanfaidh mé obair an tí níos moille.*** *I think that I will do the housework later.* ***Sílim gon-íosfaidh mé mo dhinnéar go luath.*** *I think that I will eat my dinner early.*

Tense/ Mood	Particle	Aspirate or Eclipse	Example
Conditional	*go*	Eclipse. Prefixes **n-** to vowels	***Dúirt sé godtiocfadh sé amárach.*** He said *that* he would come tomorrow. ***Déarfainn go n-osclódh siad an áit go luath.*** I would say *that* they would open the place early.
Past tense with 6 irregular verbs	*go*	Aspirate/ Eclipse	***Dúirt sé go raibh sé go luath.*** He said *that* he was early. ***Ní shílim ndeachaigh siad ar saoire.*** I don't think *that* they went on holiday. ***An síleann tú go ndearna sibh iarracht ar bith?*** Do you think *that* they didn't make any effort? ***Dúirt sé go bhfuair sé seans.*** He said *that* he didn't get a chance. ***Ní shíleann na gardaí go bhfaca siad an gadaí.*** The police don't think *that* they saw the thief. ***Ní shílim go bhfaca siad sin go fóill.*** I don't think *that* they have seen it yet.

In the examples above, the word *that* is used as a conjunction in reported speech. At other times *that* is used as a demonstrative adjective to point out something or someone out, for example, *that car, that man, that woman.* When *that* is used as an adjective it is translated into Irish by **sin**:

an gasúr sin   *that boy*

This is the same for feminine nouns:

an bhean sin   *that woman*

3.2 sula/sular

When the word *before* comes before a verb, we use either **sula** or **sular**.

Tense/Mood	Particle	Aspirate or Eclipse	Example
Past	*sular*	Aspirate	**Sular cheannaigh sé an teach bhí cónaí air in árasán.** *Before he bought the house he lived in a flat.*
Present	*sula*	Eclipse. Prefixes **n-** to vowels	**Sula dtagann sé ar ais abair leis nuachtán a fháil dom.** *Before he comes back tell him to get a newspaper for me.* **Sula n-osclaíonn tú an doras faigheochair.** *Before you open the door get a key.*
Future	*sula*	Eclipse. Prefixes **n-** to vowels	**Sula gcríochnóidh tú sin beidh tú cinnte go bhfuil sé ceart.** *Before you finish you will be sure it is right.* **Sula n-íosfaidh tú do dhinnéar nífidh do lámha.** *Before you eat your dinner you will wash your hands.*

Conditional	*sula*	Eclipse. Prefixes **n-** to vowels	*Sula n̠déanfá sin nach n̠-iarrfá cead.* *Before you do that wouldn't you ask permission?*
Past tense with 6 irregular verbs	*sula*	Aspirate/ Eclipse	*Sula raibh sé anseo bhí sé ag an siopa.* *Before he was here he was at the shop.* *Sula ndeachaigh siad ar saoire. cheannaigh siad éadaí nua.* *Before they went on holiday they bought new clothes.* *Sula n̠dearna siad an obair d'ullmhaigh siad go cúramach.* *Before they started the work they prepared carefully.* *Sula b̠hfuair sé an seans labhairt leis d'imigh an múinteoir.* *Before he got a chance to talk to him the teacher left.* *Sula bhfaca siad an scannán cheannaigh siad milseáin.* *Before they saw the film they bought sweets.* *Sula n̠dúirt siad sin ní or éist duine ar bith leo.* *Before they said that no-one listened to them.*

3.3 *mura*

This particle, in front of a verb, is the Irish for *if ... not,*:

mura dtéann tú amach anocht   *if you don't go out tonight*

Tense/ Mood	Particle	Aspirate or Eclipse	Example
Past	*murar*	Aspirate	**Murar cheannaigh sé sin, cad é a cheannaigh sé?** *If he didn't buy that, what did he buy?*
Present	*mura*	Eclipse. Prefixes *n-* to vowels	**Mura dtagann tú anois beidh fearg orm.** *If you don't come now I will be angry.* **Mura n-éistíonn liom anois ní éireoidh leat.** *If you don't listen to me now you will not succeed.*
Future	*mura*	Eclipse. Prefixes *n-* to vowels	**Mura gceannaíonn sé bia beidh ocras air.** *If he doesn't buy food he will be hungry.* **Mura n-íosfaidh glasraí ní bhfaighidh sé milseog.** *If he doesn't eat vegetables he won't get a dessert.*

Conditional	mura	Eclipse. Prefixes **n-** to vowels	**Mura <u>d</u>tiocfadh sé ní bheadh Seán sásta.** *If he weren't to come Seán wouldn't be happy.* **Mura <u>bh</u>foghlaimeofá sin ní bheadh seans sa scrúdú agat.** *If you wouldn't't learn that you would have no chance in the exam.*
Past tense with 6 irregular verbs	mura	Aspirate/ Eclipse	**Mura raibh sé ann cé eile a bhí ann?** *If he wasn't there who was there?* **Mura <u>n</u>deachaigh na páistí ar saoire is cinnte go raibh na tuismitheoirí ar saoire.** *If the children didn't go on holidays it's certain that the parents did.* **Mura <u>n</u>dearna siad sin cé a rinne é?** *If they didn't do that who did it?* **Mura bhfuair siad seal ní raibh sé sin cothrom.** *If they didn't get a turn that wasn't fair.* **Mura bhfaca tusa é cé a chonaic é?** *If you didn't see him who did see him?* **Mura ndúirt siad sin ní raibh ciall ar bith acu.** *If they didn't say that they were foolish.*

3.4 *cá/cár*

This particle is the Irish for *where* in front of a verb, for example:

Cá dtéann sé gach lá?   *Where does he go every day?*

Tense/ Mood	Particle	Aspirate or Eclipse	Example
Past	*cár*	Aspirate	**Cár m<u>h</u>úscail tú ar maidin?** *Where did you wake up this morning?*
Present	*cá*	Eclipse. Prefixes *n-* to vowels	**Cá <u>d</u>téann tú ar scoil?** *Where do you go to school?* **Cá n-ullmhaíonn an cócaire an dinnéar?** *Where does the cook prepare the dinner?*
Future	*cá*	Eclipse. Prefixes *n-* to vowels	**Cá <u>d</u>tosóidh tú ag obair?** *Where will you start working?* **Cá <u>n-</u>íocfaidh tú as an ticéad?** *Where will you pay for the ticket?*
Conditional	*cá*	Eclipse. Prefixes *n-* to vowels	**Cá gcraolfadh sé an clár as?** *Where would he broadcast the programme from?* **Cá n-íosfá dá mbeadh rogha agat?** *Where would you eat if you had the choice?*

Past tense with 6 irregular verbs	cá	Aspirate/ Eclipse	**Cá raibh tú aréir?** *Where were you last night?* **Cá _n_deachiagh tú ar saoire?** *Where did you go on holiday?* **Cá _n_dearna tú é sin?** *Where did you do that?* **Cá bhfuair tú an leabhar sin?** *Where did you get that book?* **Cá _bh_faca siad é?** *Where did they see her?* **Cá _n_dúirt siad sin an méid sin leat?** *Where did they say all that to you?*

3.5 *má* and *dá*

These are the two words in Irish used for *if* before verbs. **Má** is used when something may well happen or have happened:

má itheann tú sin   *if I see her*

and **dá** is used for less likely or hypothetical situations:

dá mbainfinn an crannchur náisiúnta   *if I won the national lottery*

Tense/ Mood	Particle	Aspirate or Eclipse	Example
Past	má	Aspirate	**Má _sh_ábháil sé airgead nuair a bhí sé óg níl rud ar bith fágtha anois aige.** *If he saved money when he was young he has none left now.*

Present/ Future	*má*	Aspirate	*Má tá sé anseo anois ní fheicim é.* If he is here now I don't see him. *Má dhéanann tú sin dom beidh mé sásta.* If you do that for me I will be happy.
Conditional	*dá*	Eclipse. Prefixes **n-** to vowels	*Dá mbainfinn milliún euro bheadh áthas an domhain orm.* If I won a million euro I would be very happy. *Dá n̲-íocfadh sé as na fiacha ar fad atá aige ní bheadh airgead ar bith fágtha aige.* If he were to pay off all his debts he would have no money left.

THE CONDITIONAL

What is the conditional mood?
The **conditional mood** is a verb form used to talk about something that may happen or that may be true, or that may have happened or may have been true depending on certain conditions: *I would go if I had permission*; *She would have won the race had she been fitter*.

1 Forming the conditional mood

1.1 Overview

➤Like other verb forms, the conditional mood is made from the base form of the verb. For the conditional we add the ending to the base form before we add the subject of the verb, if it is a pronoun.

➤When deciding what ending to add to the verb, it is important to know whether the verb is first conjugation broad or slender, or second conjugation broad or slender.

⇨ See section 2 of chapter 5 on Verbs.

➤If the verb begins with the letters *b, c, d, g, m, p, s, t* we must always aspirate in the conditional mood in **positive** and **negative** sentences but eclipse in the **question** form:

bhrisfinn	*I would break*
ní bhrisfinn	*I wouldn't break*
BUT	
an mbrisfeá?	*would you break?*

➤If the verb begins with a vowel, we place *d'* in front of the initial vowel in the conditional mood in **positive** sentences, but drop the **d'** in **negative** sentences and in the **question** form:

d'ólfainn	*I would drink*
ní ólfainn	*I wouldn't drink*
an ólfá?	*would you drink?*

➤ If the verb begins with the letter **f**, we aspirate **and** place the letter **d'** in front of the initial letter of the verb in the conditional mood in **positive** sentences, but drop the **d'** in **negative** sentences:

d'fhágfainn	*I would leave*
ní fhágfainn	*I wouldn't leave*
an bhfágfá?	*Would you leave?*

➤ In the examples which follow, the stem of each verb is given in brackets first so that we can see clearly how each stem is changed:

> ### Típ
> You should note that in the conditional mood, a lot of the pronouns are incorporated into the ending, and so do not require the pronoun to be repeated. Therefore, **ghlanfainn** means *I would clean*. The pronoun 'I' is already in the verb.

1.2 First Conjugation Verbs

➤ If the last vowel of the verb is **broad** (**a, o** or **ú**), we add:

fainn	*I*
fá	*you*
fadh sé	*he*
fadh sí	*she*

faimis	we
fadh sibh	you (plural)
faidís	they

dún *close*

Dhúnfainn an doras dá mbeadh an eochair agam.   I would lock the door if I had the key.

scríobh *write*

Scríobhfadh sí litir dá mbeadh peann aici.   She would write a letter if she had a pen.

ol *drink*

D'ólfaimis tae dá mbeadh sé ar fáil.   We would drink tea if it were available.

➤ If the last vowel of the verb is **slender** (*i*), we add:

finn	I
feá	you
feadh sé	he
feadh sí	she
fimis	we
feadh sibh	you (plural)
fidís	they

eist *listen*

D'éistfinn le ceol dá mbeadh raidió agam.   I would listen to music if I had a radio.

bris *break*

> **Bhris<u>feadh</u> siad isteach sa teach**   *They would break into the house if*
> **muna mbeadh eochair acu.**   *they hadn't got a key.*

➤ If the verb ends in **-áil** or **-áin**, we remove the letter **i** before adding the **broad** endings:

fainn	I
fá	you
fadh sé	he
fadh sí	she
faimis	we
fadh sibh	you (plural)
faidís	they

taispeáin *show*

> **Thaispeán<u>faimis</u> dóibh an**   *We would show them the new*
> **teach nua dá n-iarrfaidís é.**   *house if they asked.*

1.3 Second conjugation verbs

➤ If the verb ends in **-aigh**, we *remove* the **-aigh** and add the following **broad** endings:

óinn	I
ófá	you
ódh sé	he
ódh sí	she
óimis	we
ódh sibh	you (plural)
óidís	they

ceannaigh buy

> **Cheann<u>ó</u>inn gluaisteán nua dá**   *I would buy a new car if I had*
> **mbeadh an t-airgead agam.**   *the money.*

brostaigh hurry

> **Bhrost<u>óidís</u> abhaile dá mbeadh**   *They would hurry home if it was*
> **sé fuar.**   *cold.*

➤ If the verb ends in **-igh**, we *remove* the **-igh** and add the following
slender endings:

eoinn	*I*
eofá	*you*
eodh sé	*he*
eodh sí	*she*
eoimis	*we*
eodh sibh	*you* (plural)
eoidís siad	*they*

eirigh get up

> **D'éir<u>eoinn</u> go luath dá mbeadh**   *I would get up early if I had a job.*
> **post agam.**

oibrigh work

> **D'oibr<u>eodh</u> sí go dian dá**   *She would work hard if she got*
> **mbeadh an tuarastal ceart**   *a proper wage.*
> **aici.**

➤ If the verb has more than one syllable and is broad (ends in **-ail,**
-ain or **-ais**), we remove the **-ai** and add the **broad** endings:

óinn	I
ófá	you
ódh sé	he
ódh sí	she
óimis	we
ódh sibh	you (plural)
óidís	they

múscail wake up

Mhúscl<u>ódh</u> sí go luath gach maidin dá mbeadh clog aláraim aici.	She would wake up every morning if she had an alarm clock.

oscail open

D'oscl<u>óimis</u> an teach tábhairne gach oíche dá mbeadh ceadúnas again.	We would open the pub every night if we had a licence.

➤ If the verb has more than one syllable and is slender (ends in **-il, -in** or **-is**), we remove the **-i**, and add the **slender** endings:

eoinn	I
eofá	you
eodh sé	he
eodh sí	she
eoimis	we
eodh sibh	you (plural)
eoidís	they

imir play

> **D'imreoinn peil le mo chara dá**   *I would play football with my friend if*
> **mbeadh cead agam.**   *I was allowed.*

2   Asking and answering questions with verbs in the conditional mood

➤To ask questions in the conditional mood, we put **an** before the verb, and eclipse the first letter of the verb. Verbs beginning with vowels **are not** eclipsed.

brisfeadh sé	*he would break*
an mbrisfeadh sé?	*would he break?*
ólfadh siad	*they would drink*
an ólfadh siad?	*would they drink?*

➤To answer in the negative in the conditional, we put **ní** before the conditional verb, and aspirate the first letter of the verb. **Ní** does nothing to words beginning with vowels:

ní bhrisfeadh sé	*he wouldn't break*
ní ólfadh siad	*they wouldn't drink*

3   Irregular verbs in the conditional mood

➤ Some irregular verbs change in the conditional mood

	Conditional	Negative	Question
bí be	**bheinn** *I would be*	*ní bheinn*	*an mbeinnan*
	bheifeá *you would be*	*ní bheifeá*	*an mbeifeáan*
	bheadh sé *he would be*	*ní bheadh sé*	*an mbeadh sé*
	bheadh sí *she would be*	*ní bheadh sí*	*an mbeadh sí*
	bheimis *we would be*	*ní bheimis*	*an mbeimis*
	bheadh sibh *you would be*	*ní bheadh sibh*	*an mbeadh sibh*
	bheidís *they would be*	*ní bheidís*	*an mbeidís*
tar come	**thiocfainn** *I would come*	*ní thiocfainn*	*an dtiocfainn*
	thiocfá *you would come*	*ní thiocfá*	*an dtiocfá*
	thiocfadh sé *he would come*	*ní thiocfadh sé*	*an dtiocfadh sé*
	thiocfadh sí *she would come*	*ní thiocfadh sí*	*an dtiocfadh sí*
	thiocfaimis *we would come*	*ní thiocfaimis*	*an dtiocfaimis*
	thiocfadh sibh *you would come*	*ní thiocfadh sibh*	*an dtiocfadh sibh*
	thiocfaidís *they would come*	*ní thiocfaidís*	*an dtiocfaidís*

	Conditional	Negative	Question
téigh go	**rachainn** *I would go*	*ní rachainn*	*an rachainn*
	rachfá *you would go*	*ní rachfá*	*an rachfá*
	rachadh sé *he would go*	*ní rachadh sé*	*an rachadh sé*
	rachadh sí *she would go*	*ní rachadh sí*	*an rachadh sí*
	rachaimis *we would go*	*ní rachaimis*	*an rachaimis*
	rachadh sibh *you would go*	*ní rachadh sibh*	*an rachadh sibh*
	rachaidís *they would go*	*ní rachaidís*	*an rachaidís*
feic see	**d'fheicfinn** *I would see*	*ní fheicfinn*	*an bhfeicfinn*
	d'fheicfeá *you would see*	*ní fheicfeá*	*an bhfeicfeá*
	d'fheicfeadh sé *he would see*	*ní fheicfeadh sé*	*an bhfeicfeadh sé*
	d'fheicfeadh sí *she would see*	*ní fheicfeadh sí*	*an bhfeicfeadh sí*
	d'fheicfimis *we would see*	*ní fheicfimis*	*an bhfeicfimis*
	d'fheicfeadh sibh *you would see*	*ní fheicfeadh sibh*	*an bhfeicfeadh sibh*
	d'fheicfidís *they would see*	*ní fheicfidís*	*an bhfeicfidís*

	Conditional	Negative	Question
clois hear	chloisfinn *I would hear*	*ní chloisfinn*	*an gcloisfinn*
	chloisfeá *you would hear*	*ní chloisfeá*	*an gcloisfeá*
	chloisfeadh sé *he would hear*	*ní chloisfeadh sé*	*an gcloisfeadh sé*
	chloisfeadh sí *she would hear*	*ní chloisfeadh sí*	*an gcloisfeadh sí*
	chloisfimis *we would hear*	*ní chloisfimis*	*an gcloisfimis*
	chloisfeadh sibh *you would hear*	*ní chloisfeadh sibh*	*an gcloisfeadh sibh*
	chloisfidís *they would hear*	*ní chloisfidís*	*an gcloisfidís*
abair say	**déarfainn** *I would say*	*ní dhéarfainn*	*an ndéarfainn*
	déarfá *you would say*	*ní dhéarfá*	*an ndéarfá*
	déarfadh sé *he would say*	*ní dhéarfadh sé*	*an ndéarfadh sé*
	déarfadh sí *she would say*	*ní dhéarfadh sí*	*an ndéarfadh sí*
	déarfaimis *we would say*	*ní dhéarfaimis*	*an ndéarfaimis*
	déarfadh sibh *you would say*	*ní dhéarfadh sibh*	*an ndéarfadh sibh*
	déarfaidís *they would say*	*ní dhéarfaidís*	*an ndéarfaidís*

	Conditional	Negative	Question
déan do/ make	dhéanfainn I would do/make	ní dhéanfainn	an ndéanfainn
	dhéanfá you would do/make	ní dhéanfá	an ndéanfá
	dhéanfadh sé he would do/make	ní dhéanfadh sé	an ndéanfadh sé
	dhéanfadh sí she would do/make	ní dhéanfadh sí	an ndéanfadh sí
	dhéanfaimis we would do/make	ní dhéanfaimis	an ndéanfaimis
	dhéanfadh sibh you would do/make	ní dhéanfadh sibh	an ndéanfadh sibh
	dhéanfaidís they would do/make	ní dhéanfaidís	an ndéanfaidís
beir grab	bhéarfainn I would grab	ní bhéarfainn	an mbéarfainn
	bhéarfá you would grab	ní bhéarfá	an mbéarfá
	bhéarfadh sé he would grab	ní bhéarfadh sé	an mbéarfadh sé
	bhéarfadh sí she would grab	ní bhéarfadh sí	an mbéarfadh sí
	bhéarfaimis we would grab	ní bhéarfaimis	an mbéarfaimis
	bhéarfadh sibh you would grab	ní bhéarfadh sibh	an mbéarfadh sibh
	bhéarfaidís they would grab	ní bhéarfaidís	an mbéarfaidís

	Conditional	Negative	Question
faigh get	gheobhainn *I would get*	ní bhfaighinn	an bhfaighinn
	gheofá *you would get*	ní bhfaighfeá	an bhfaighfeá
	gheobhadh sé *he would get*	ní bhfaigheadh sé	an bhfaigheadh sé
	gheobhadh sí *she would get*	ní bhfaigheadh sí	an bhfaigheadh sí
	gheobhaimis *we would get*	ní bhfaighimis	an bhfaighimis
	gheobhadh sibh *you would get*	ní bhfaigheadh sibhní	an bhfaigheadh sibh
	gheobhaidís *they would get*	bhfaighidís	an bhfaighidís
tabhair give	thabharfainn *I would give*	ní thabharfainn	an dtabharfainn
	thabharfá *you would give*	ní thabharfá	an dtabharfá
	thabharfadh sé *he would give*	ní thabharfadh sé	an dtabharfadh sé
	thabharfadh sí *she would give*	ní thabharfadh sí	an dtabharfadh sí
	thabharfaimis *we would give*	ní thabharfaimis	an dtabharfaimisan
	thabharfadh sibh *you would give*	ní thabharfadh sibh	dtabharfadh sibh
	thabharfaidís *they would give*	ní thabharfaidís	an dtabharfaidís

	Conditional	Negative	Question
ith eat	d'íosfainn I would eat	ní íosfainn	an íosfainn
	d'íosfá you would eat	ní íosfá	an íosfá
	d'íosfadh sé he would eat	ní íosfadh sé	an íosfadh sé
	d'íosfadh sí she would eat	ní íosfadh sí	an íosfadh sí
	d'íosfaimis we would eat	ní íosfaimis	an íosfaimis
	d'íosfadh sibh you would eat	ní íosfadh sibh	an íosfadh sibh
	d'íosfaidís they would eat	ní íosfaidís	an íosfaidís

Típ

To express the conditional in the past tense, ie *I would have done that*, we use the conditional as above.

THE PASSIVE

What is the passive?
The **passive voice in Irish** is the form of the verb which is used when we are unaware of the subject of the sentence, or we choose not to say who or what the subject is, for example, *the window was broken; the work will be done*. Irish differs from English in the sense that we cannot have phrases like *The window was broken by Orlaith*. In translating this to Irish we must say **Bhris Orlaith an fhuinneog** *Orlaith broke the window*.

1 Forming the passive

1.1 Overview

➤ The passive is formed from the base form of the verb. We add an ending to the base form of the verb.

➤ When deciding what ending to add to the verb to form the passive, it is important to know whether the verb is first conjugation broad or slender, or second conjugation broad or slender.

⇨   See section 2 of chapter 5 on Verbs.

➤ The passive appears in all tenses.

➤ The positive passive form is always aspirated in the conditional:

d<u>h</u>éanfaí an obair   *the work would be done*

➤ The passive is neither aspirated nor eclipsed in the past tense at any time:

Briseadh an fhuinneog.	*The window was broken.*
Níor briseadh an fhuinneog.	*The window wasn't broken.*
Ar briseadh an fhuinnneog	*Was the window broken?*

➤**D'** is always removed in from verbs beginning with a vowel or the letter **f** plus a vowel in the past tense.

| **Ullmhaíodh an dinnéar.** | *The dinner was prepared.* |
| **Fágadh an gasúr ina aonar.** | *The boy was left alone.* |

1.2 First conjugation verbs

➤If the last vowel of the verb is **broad** (**a, o** or **ú**), we add:

Past:	-adh
Present:	-tar
Future:	-far
Conditional:	-faí

tóg lift/build

| **Tógadh an teach go gasta.** | *The house was built quickly.* |
| **Thógfaí an teach dá mbeadh an t-airgead again.** | *The house would be built if we had the money.* |

glan clean

| **Glantar na leithris gach lá.** | *The toilets are cleaned every day.* |

íoc pay

| **Locfar an bille in am.** | *The bill will be paid in time* |

➤ If the last vowel of the verb is **slender** (*i*), we add:

Past:	*-eadh*
Present:	*-tear*
Future:	*-fear*
Conditional:	*-fí*

bris *break*

> **Bris<u>eadh</u> isteach sa teach sin aréir.**
> *That house was broken into last night.*

eist *listen*

> **Éis<u>tear</u> le ceol traidisiúnta in Éirinn.**
> *Traditional music is listened to in Ireland.*

cuir *put*

> **Cuir<u>fear</u> an fhoireann amach as an chomórtas.**
> *The team will be put out of the competition.*

mill *destroy*

> **Mhill<u>fí</u> an dinnéar dá bhfágfaí amuigh é.**
> *The dinner would be destroyed if it were left out.*

➤ If the verb ends in **-áil** or **-áin**, we remove the letter **i** before adding the **broad** endings:

Past:	*-adh*
Present:	*-tar*
Future:	*-far*
Conditional:	*-faí*

taispeáin *show*

> **Taispeán<u>adh</u> scannán aréir.**   A film was shown last night.

sábháil *save*

> **Sábháil<u>tear</u> airgead gach bliain.**   Money is saved every year.

sóinseáil *change*

> **Sóinseál<u>far</u> do chuid airgid sa bhanc.**   Your money will be changed in the bank.

tástáil *test*

> **T<u>h</u>ástál<u>faí</u> an gluaisteán sin dá mbeadh an garáiste oscailte.**   That car would be tested if the garage were open.

1.3 Second conjugation verbs

➤ If the verb ends in **-aigh**, we *remove* the **-aigh** and add the following **broad** endings:

Past:	-aíodh
Present:	-aítear
Future:	-ófar
Conditional:	-ófaí

ceannaigh *buy*

> **Ceann<u>aíodh</u> an teach ar leathphraghas.**   The house was bought at half price.

eagraigh *organize*

> **Eagr<u>aítear</u> imeachtaí go minic.**   Events are organized often.

beannaigh *bless*

> **Beann<u>ófar</u> an leanbh sin.**   *That child will be blessed.*

ceartaigh *correct*

> **Cheart<u>ófaí</u> an obair dá**   *The work would be corrected if the*
> **mbeadh an múinteoir**   *teacher were at school.*
> **ar scoil.**

➤ If the verb ends in **-igh**, we *remove* the **-igh** and add the following **slender** endings:

Past:	-íodh
Present:	-ítear
Future:	-eofar
Conditional:	-eofaí

bailigh *collect*

> **Bail<u>íodh</u> cuid mhór airgid inné.**   *A lot of money was collected*
>   *yesterday.*

dúisigh *wake up*

> **Dúis<u>ítear</u> na páistí sin go luath.**   *Those children are woken up early.*

dírigh *direct*

> **Dír<u>eofar</u> aird ar na**   *Attention will be directed to the*
> **polaiteoirí anois.**   *politicians now.*

sínigh *sign*

> **Shín<u>eofaí</u> an litir dá mbeadh**   *The letter would be signed if it were*
> **sí scríofa mar is ceart.**   *written properly.*

➤ If the verb has more than one syllable and is broad (ends in **-ail**, **-ain** or **-ais**), we *remove* the **-ai** and add the **broad** endings:

Past:	*-aíodh*
Present:	*aítear*
Future:	*-ófar*
Conditional:	*-ófaí*

múscail   *wake up*

> **Múscla<u>aíodh</u> na saighdiúirí go luath.**

> *The soldiers were woken up early.*

> **Múscl<u>ófar</u> maidin amárach thú ar a hocht.**

> *You will be woken up tomorrow morning at 8.*

oscail   *open*

> **Oscl<u>aítear</u> an doras ag an am chéanna gach lá.**

> *The door is opened at the same time every day.*

cosain   *defend*

> **<u>Ch</u>osn<u>ófaí</u> an tír seo dá ndéanfaí ionsaí uirth.**

> *This country would be defended if it were attacked.*

➤If the verb has more than one syllable and is slender (ends in **-il, -in** or **-is**), we *remove* the **-i** and add the **slender** endings:

Past:	*-íodh*
Present:	*-ítear*
Future:	*-eofar*
Conditional:	*-eofaí*

imir   *play*

> **Imr<u>íodh</u> an cluiche inné cé go raibh sé ag cur.**

> *The game was played yesterday even though it was raining.*

eitil fly

> **Eitlítear an t-eitleán ó Ghlaschú go Béal Feirste gach lá..**

The plane is flown from Glasgow to Belfast every day.

coigil save

> **Coigleofar a lán airgid sa chéad cháinaisnéis eile.**

A lot of money will be saved in the next budget.

inis tell

> **D'inseofaí an fhírinne mura mbeadh eagla ar dhaoine.**

The truth would be told if people weren't afraid.

2 Asking and answering questions with verbs in the passive

➤ To ask questions in the passive, we follow the same rules as for other tenses. The only difference is that **ar** never aspirates in the past tense.

With subject:

> **Ar dhíol an fear an teach go fóill?**   *Has the man sold the house yet?*

Irish passive (without subject):

> **Ar díoladh an teach go fóill?**   *Has the house been sold yet?*

➤ To answer in the negative in the future tense, we follow the same rules as for the other tenses. The only difference is that **níor** never aspirates in the past tense.

With subject:

> **Níor bhris Caoimhín na rialacha.**   *Caoimhín didn't break the rules.*

Irish passive (without subject):

> **Níor briseadh na rialacha.**   *The rules weren't broken.*

3 The passive with irregular verbs

Some irregular verbs change in the conditional

	Past	Present	Future	Conditional
bí be	bhíothas ní rabhthas an rabhthas nach rabhthas go rabhthas	bítear ní bhítear an mbítear nach mbítear go mbítear	beifear ní bheifear an mbeifear nach mbeifear go mbeifear	bheifí ní bheifí an mbeifí nach mbeifí go mbeifí
clois hear	chualathas níor chualathas ar chualathas nár chualathas gur chualathas	cluintear ní chluintear an gcluintear nach gcluintear go gcluintear	cluinfear ní chluinfear an gcluinfear nach gcluinfear go gcluinfear	chluinfí ní chluinfí an gcluinfí nach gcluinfí go gcluinfí
déan do/ make	rinneadh ní dhearnadh an ndearnadh nach ndearnadh go ndearnadh	déantar ní dhéantar an ndéantar nach ndéantar go ndéantar	déanfar ní dhéanfar an ndéanfar nach ndéanfar go ndéanfar	dhéanfaí ní dhéanfaí an ndéanfaí nach ndéanfaí go ndéanfaí
abair say	dúradh ní dúradh an ndúradh nach ndúradh go ndúradh	deirtear ní deirtear an ndeirtear nach ndeirtear go ndeirtear	déarfar ní déarfar an ndéarfar nach ndéarfar go ndéarfar	déarfaí ní déarfaí an ndéarfaí nach ndéarfaí go ndéarfaí
faigh get	fuarthas ní bhfuarthas an bhfuarthas nach bhfuarthas go bhfuarthas	faightear ní fhaightear an bhfaightear nach bhfaightear go bhfaightear	gheobhfar ní bhfaighfear an bhfaighfear nach bhfaighfear go bhfaighfear	gheobhfaí ní bhfaighfí an bhfaighfí nach bhfaighfí go bhfaighfí
feic see	chonacthas ní fhacthas an bhfacthas nach bhfacthas go bhfacthas	feictear ní fheictear an bhfeictear nach bhfeictear go bhfeictear	feicfear ní fheicfear an bhfeicfear nach bhfeicfear go bhfeicfear	d'fheicfí ní fheicfí an bhfeicfí nach bhfeicfí go bhfeicfí
ith eat	itheadh níor itheadh ar itheadh nár itheadh gur itheadh	itear ní itear an itear nach n-itear go n-itear	íosfar ní íosfar an íosfar nach n-íosfar go n-íosfar	d'íosfaí ní íosfaí an íosfaí nach n-íosfaí go n-íosfaí

	Past	Present	Future	Conditional
tabhair give	tugadh níor tugadh ar tugadh nár tugadh gur tugadh	tugtar ní thugtar an dtugtar nach dtugtar go dtugtar	tabharfar ní thabharfar an dtabharfar nach dtabharfar go dtabharfar	thabharfaí ní thabharfaí an dtabharfaí nach dtabharfaí go dtabharfaí
tar come	thángthas níor thángthas ar thángthas nár thángthas gur thángthas	tagtar ní thagtar an dtagar nach dtagtar go dtagtar	tiocfar ní thiocfar an dtiocfar nach dtiocfar go dtiocfar	thiocfaí ní thiocfaí an dtiocfaí nach dtiocfaí go dtiocfaí
téigh go	chuathas ní dheachthas an ndeachthas nach ndeachthas go ndeachthas	téitear ní théitear an dtéitear nach dtéitear go dtéitear	rachfar ní rachfar an rachfar nach rachfar go rachfar	rachfaí ní rachfaí an rachfaí nach rachfaí go rachfaí
bei grab	rugadh níor rugadh ar rugadh nár rugadh gur rugadh	beirtear ní bheirtear an mbeirtear nach mbeirtear go mbeirtear	béarfar ní bhéarfar an mbéarfar nach mbéarfar go mbéarfar	bhéarfaí ní bhéarfaí an mbéarfaí nach mbéarfaí go mbéarfaí

KEY POINTS

✔ The Irish passive is used when we don't know or don't want to say who or what carries out the action of the verb.

✔ The passive is formed from the stem of the verb.

✔ Neither **níor** nor **ar** aspirates the passive in the past tense.

THE SUBJUNCTIVE

What is the subjunctive mood?
The subjunctive mood is a verb form used to express a wish or an action that has not yet occurred, for example, *May he never return*. The subjunctive mood is rarely used now in Irish, but it is still found in certain situations, especially in prayers and blessings.

1 Using the subjunctive

There are three main uses of the subjunctive mood in Irish: to express a wish, to express purpose and to express uncertainty.

1.1 Expressing a wish

go comes before the verb in positive sentences and eclipses, and *nár* comes before the verb in negative sentences and aspirates. **Go raibh, ná raibh** are the forms of the verb *bí to be*, and the most commonly heard term is:

> **go raibh maith agat** *thank you*

this literally means "may you have good".

> **Go dtaga an lá nuair a bheidh mé pósta.** *May the day come when I am married.*
>
> **Nár fhile an fear sin arís anseo.** *May that man never come back here.*

1.2   Expressing purpose after *go, nó go, sula*

Rachaidh mé ann go bhfeice mé é.	*I will go there to see him (lit. so I will see him).*
Fan go dtaga mo chara ar ais.	*Wait until my friend comes back.*
Bí ar ais anseo sula dté sé abhaile.	*Be back here before he goes home.*

1.3   Expressing uncertainty after *mura*

Cad é a dhéanfaimid mura dtaga do mháthair ar ais?	*What will we do if your mother does not come back?*
Mura gcreide sibh mé ná héist liom.	*If you don't believe me don't listen to me.*

2   Forming the subjunctive

As with other tenses and moods in Irish, the subjunctive is formed from the stem of the verb.

2.1   First conjugation verbs

➤If the verb is broad, we add **-a**, and if it is slender, we add **-e**:

mol (*praise*)	**bris** (*break*)
mola mé	brise mé
mola tú	brise tú
mola sé	brise sé
mola sí	brise sí
molaimid	brisimid
mola sibh	brise sibh
mola siad	brise siad

➤If the verb ends in **-áil**, we drop the **i** and add **a**, and if it ends in **-áin**, we add **e**:

reáchtáil (*organize*)	**tiomáin** (*drive*)
reáchtála mé	tiomáine mé
reáchtála tú	tiomáine tú
reáchtála sé	tiomáine sé
reáchtála sí	tiomáine sí
reáchtálaimid	tiomáinimid
reáchtála sibh	tiomáine sibh
reáchtála siad	tiomáine siad

2.2 Second conjugation verbs

➤If the verb ends in **-aigh**, we change **-aigh** to **-aí**, and if it ends in **-igh**, we change **-igh** to **-í**:

ceannaigh (buy)	**cruinnigh** (collect)
ceannaí mé	cruinní mé
ceannaí tú	cruinní tú
ceannaí sé	cruinní sé
ceannaí sí	cruinní sí
ceannaimid	cruinnimid
ceannaí sibh	cruinní sibh
ceannaí siad	cruinní siad

➤If the verb ends in **-air**, we change **-air** to **-raí**, and if it ends in **-ir**, we change **-ir** to **-rí**:

labhair (speak)	**imir** (play)
labhraí mé	imrí mé
labhraí tú	imrí tú
labhraí sé	imrí sé
labhraí sí	imrí sí
labhraimid	imrímid
labhraí sibh	imrí sibh
labhraí siad	imrí siad

KEY POINTS

✔ The subjunctive is not commonly used in Irish.
✔ The subjunctive is used to express wish, purpose and uncertainty.
✔ It is usually preceded by *go, sula, nó go, mura* or *nár*.

ADVERBS

What is an adverb?

An adverb is a word that gives more information about a verb, an adjective or another adverb. If we look at the sentence *Mary runs quickly*, '*quickly*' describes how Mary runs. In the sentence *Mary runs very fast*, '*very*' describes the adverb '*quickly*' and gives information about how quickly Mary runs.

There are three main types of adverbs in Irish:

1. Adverbs which are formed from adjectives
2. Adverbs of time
3. Adverbs of direction

1   Adverbs which are formed from adjectives

➤Normally, to form an adverb from an adjective, we put **go** in front of it:

fear maith	a good man
Rinne tú <u>go maith</u> é.	You did it <u>well</u>.
ceol ciúin	quiet music
Cheol an cailín <u>go ciúin</u>.	The girl sang <u>quietly</u>.

➤**go** places **h** in front of adjectives beginning with a vowel to form adverbs:

cluiche iontach	a wonderful game
D'imir sé <u>go hiontach</u>.	He played <u>wonderfully</u>.

2 Adverbs of time

The adverbs of time are never changed:

feasta	from now on
anois	now
fós	yet, still
go fóill	yet, still
inné	yesterday
amárach	tomorrow
inniu	today
ar maidin	in the morning
láithreach	immediately
fadó	long ago
anuraidh	last year

➤*riamh*   never (this is used in the past tense):

Ní raibh mé <u>riamh</u> in Albain.	I have never been to Scotland.
An raibh tú riamh sa Fhrainc?	Have you ever been in France?

➤*choíche*   never (this is used in the future tense):

Ní rachaidh mé ann <u>choíche.</u>	I will never go there.
An dtiocfaidh siad <u>choíche?</u>	Will they never come?

➤*seo chugainn*   next (in reference to days, weeks and months):

an tseachtain <u>seo chugainn</u>	next week
an mhí <u>seo chugainn</u>	next month

an Mháirt _seo chugainn_   _next Tuesday_

➤ **seo caite/seo a chuaigh thart** (in reference to days, weeks and months):

an deireadh seachtaine   _last weekend_
   seo caite/seo a chuaigh thart

an Satharn _seo caite/_   _last Saturday_
   seo a chuaigh thart

3   Adverbs of direction

3.1 Out and in

There are two words in Irish for *out* and *in*. One refers to the direction you are going and the other refers to your final position.

➤ *amach* (direction)**/amuigh** (final position)   *out*:

Téann sé <u>amach</u>.	He goes out.
Tá sé <u>amuigh</u>.	He is out.
Rachaidh mé <u>amach</u> anois.	I will go out now.
Beidh mé <u>amuigh</u> ansin.	I will be out then.

➤ *isteach* (direction)**/istigh** (final position)   *in*:

Chuaigh mé <u>isteach</u>.	I went in.
Bhí mé <u>istigh</u>.	I was in.
Rachaidh sí <u>isteach</u>.	She comes in.
Beidh sí <u>istigh</u>.	She will be in.

3.2 Up and down

A similar system applies for the words for *up* and *down* in Irish, and the word we use depends on the direction from which we are coming and the position from which we are starting. A very easy way to learn this is to think of being in the middle of a staircase.

suas	*up*	(going up)
thuas	*up*	(when you have reached the top)
anuas	*down*	(coming down from a high position)

síos	*down*	(going down)
thíos	*down*	(when you have reached the bottom)
aníos	*up*	(coming up from a lower position)

Téigh <u>suas</u> an staighre.	*Go up the stairs.*
Tá an fear <u>thuas</u> san áiléar.	*The man is up in the attic.*
Thit an pictiúr <u>anuas</u> den bhalla.	*The picture fell down off the wall.*
Téigh <u>síos</u> go bun an.	*Go down to the bottom of the ladder.*
Fan <u>thíos</u> ag bun an dréimire.	*Wait down at the bottom of the ladder.*
Tar <u>aníos</u> as an siléar.	*Come up from the cellar.*

3.3 The points of the compass

an tuaisceart	an deisceart	an toirthear	an tIarthar
the north	*the south*	*the east*	*the west*
ó thuaidh	**ó dheas**	**soir**	**siar**
northwards	*southwards*	*eastwards*	*westwards*
aduaidh	**aneas**	**anois**	**aniar**
from the north	*from the south*	*from the east*	*from the west*
thuaidh	**aduaidh**	**thoir**	**thiar**
in the north	*in the south*	*in the east*	*in the west*

If, for example, you were travelling from Newry (in the east of Ireland) to Galway (in the west of Ireland), you would say:

Tá an Ghaillimh san Iarthar.	*Galway is in the West.*
Chuaigh muid siar go Gaillimh.	*We went west(wards) to Galway.*
Tá An tIúr san Oirthear.	*Newry is in the East.*
Chuaigh muid soir chun an Iúir.	*We went East(wards) to Newry.*

KEY POINTS

✔ Adverbs give additional information about verbs, adjectives or other adverbs.
✔ The main adverbs in Irish are adverbs which are formed from adjectives, adverbs of time and adverbs of direction.
✔ When dealing with the adverbs *up* and *down*, *in* and *out*, and *directions*, the English word has more than one possible translation.

PREPOSITIONS

What is a preposition?
A preposition is a word that comes before a noun or pronoun and is used to link that noun or pronoun to something else in a sentence.

1 Simple and compound prepositions

- There are two types of prepositions in Irish: **simple prepositions** and **compound prepositions**.

- Simple prepositions have one element. Some of them aspirate the noun that follows them, others eclipse it and some make no change to it.

Tá an leabhar <u>ar</u> an tábla.	The book is <u>on</u> the table.
Tá an gasúr i dteach éigin.	The boy is <u>in</u> some house.
Tá an airgead <u>ag</u> Seán.	Seán has money.

- The noun that follows simple prepositions is in the dative case.

- The simple prepositions in Irish are as follows:

ag	*at*
ar	*on*
as	*out of*
chuig	*to*
de	*of*
do	*to*
faoi	*under*
gan	*without*
go	*to*

i	*in*
idir	*between*
ionsar	*towards*
le	*with*
mar	*like*
ó	*from*
roimh	*before*
seachas	*except*
thar	*over*
um	*about*

- Compound prepositions have more than one element and the noun that follows them must be put into the genitive case.

Tá sé <u>ar aghaidh</u> an dorais.	*It is opposite the door.*
Chuaigh <u>sé ar chúl</u> an tí.	*He went behind the house.*
Imríonn sé <u>i lár na</u> páirce.	*He plays in the middle of the field.*

- Some of the compound prepositions in Irish are as follows:

ar aghaidh	*opposite*
ar chúl	*behind*
ar fud	*throughout*
de chois	*near*
faoi bhun	*under*
i lár	*in the middle of*
i measc	*among*
in aice	*near*
os cionn	*above*
os comhair	*before*
ar feadh	*for*
tar éis	*after*
i rith	*during*
de bharr	*because of*
le haghaidh	*for*
i mbun	*in charge of*

2   Changes caused by simple prepositions to nouns beginning with a consonant

Different prepositions have different effects on nouns that start with a consonant. We can split them up according to the effect they have.

➤ *ag, as, le, chuig, go, seachas*

- These prepositions have no effect on the noun that follows them.

Tá gluaisteán deas __ag__ fear an phoist.	*The postman has a nice car.*
__As__ Baile Átha Cliath ó dhúchas mé.	*I am from Dublin originally.*
Tháinig mé __le__ cara.	*I came with a friend.*
Cuir sin __chuig__ duine éigin.	*Send that to someone.*
An dtiocfaidh tú liom __go__ Doire ar maidin?	*Will you come to Derry with me in the morning?*
Bhí gach duine ann __seachas__ Peadar.	*Everyone was there except Peadar.*

➤ *de, do, faoi, mar, ó, roimh, um*

- These prepositions aspirate nouns if possible.

Tá mé lán de dhóchas.	*I am full of hope.*
Thug mé airgead do Sheán.	*I gave some money to Seán.*
Ar chuala tú faoi Chormac?	*Did you hear about Cormac?*
Beidh mé ag imirt mar chúl báire.	*I will be playing full-back.*
ó thús na bliana	*from the beginning of the year*

Bhí sé sa teach roimh Mhicheál.	*He was in the house before Mícheál.*
trí ph̲oll na heochrach	*through the keyhole*

[i] Remember some consonants cannot be aspirated. In this case the prepositions above have no effect.

➤*ar*

- The preposition **ar** behaves in different ways depending on its meaning in the sentence.

- It aspirates nouns when they indicate a general situation.

Tá cóta ar Sh̲eán.	*Seán is wearing a coat.*
Tá áthas ar Sh̲íle gur éirigh léi.	*Síle is happy that she passed.*

- It doesn't aspirate nouns when they portray general position.

Bhí an gasúr ar d̲eireadh.	*The boy was at the back.*
Bhí gach duine ar b̲ord.	*Everybody was on board.*

- It doesn't aspirate nouns when they portray a state or a condition.

Bhí sé ar m̲eisce.	*He was drunk.*
Fuair sé an post ar c̲onradh.	*He got the job on contract.*

- It doesn't aspirate nouns that follow when they are related to time.

Feicfidh mé ar b̲all thú.	*I'll see you later.*
Beidh Peadar ann ar m̲aidin.	*Peadar will be there in the morning.*

➤*gan*

- *gan* aspirates nouns if they are on their own (if they have no adjective or other information attached) and don't begin with **f, d** or **t**.

Tá tú gan m<u>h</u>aith.	*You are useless.*
Tá tú gan c<u>h</u>iall.	*You are stupid.*

  But

Chuaigh sé ann gan <u>p</u>ingin <u>rua</u>.	*He went without a penny.*
Abair leis gan <u>m</u>ála <u>a thógáil.</u>	*Tell him not to lift a bag.*
Bhí mé gan <u>f</u>reagra.	*I didn't have an answer.*

- Nouns are not aspirated after *gan* if they are a person's name.

Tháinig sé gan <u>M</u>icheál.	*He came without Micheál.*

➤*idir*

- *idir* aspirates nouns when it means *between* or *both*.

Bhí idir <u>gh</u>asúir agus <u>gh</u>irseacha sa scoil.	*There were both boys and girls in the school.*
Bhí idir <u>ch</u>airde agus <u>gh</u>aolta ar an mbainis.	*Both friends and relations were at the wedding.*

- *idir* aspirates nouns when it indicates space in distance or time.

Tá 100 míle idir <u>B</u>éal Feirste agus Baile Átha Cliath.	*There are 100 miles between Belfast and Dublin.*
Bíonn sé ar saoire idir Bealtaine agus Meán Fómhair.	*He is on holiday between May and September.*

➤ *thar*

- *thar* aspirates nouns most of the time.

  Ní raibh thar b<u>h</u>eirt ann.   *There weren't more than two people there.*

  Chuaigh sé thar b<u>h</u>arr   *He went over the top of the hill.*
  an chnoic.

➤ *i*

- Nouns are eclipsed after *i*.

  Tá mé i mo chónaí i   *I live in Westport.*
  <u>g</u>Cathair na Mart.

  Cuir i <u>m</u>bosca é.   *Put it in a box.*

> 🛈 Remember some consonants cannot be eclipsed. In this case the prepositions above have no effect.

3 Changes caused by simple prepositions to nouns beginning with a vowel

Different prepositions have different effects on nouns that start with a vowel. We can split them up according to the effect that they have.

➤*ag, ar, as, chuig, faoi, gan, idir, mar, ó, roimh, seachas, thar, trí, um*

No changes are made to nouns after these prepositions.

Tá milseáin ag <u>S</u>eán.	*Seán has got sweets.*
Tá sé ina luí ar <u>u</u>rlár an tseomra.	*It is on the floor of the room.*
Tá an madra sin gan <u>a</u>inm.	*That dog has no name.*
Fuair mé ó <u>Ú</u>na é.	*I got it from Úna.*
Ní raibh thar <u>o</u>chtar ann.	*There weren't more than eight there.*

➤*go, le*

These prepositions place an **h** before nouns.

Tá sé ag dul go <u>h</u>Ard Mhacha.	*He is going to Armagh.*
Ná labhair le <u>h</u>Éamonn.	*Don't speak to Éamonn.*

➤*de, do*

The **-e** of **de** and the **-o** of **do** are lost before a vowel and before **fh** and an apostrophe is added in their place.

Thug sé an t-airgead <u>d</u>'Úna.	*He gave Úna the money.*
Bhain sé an craiceann <u>d</u>'oráiste.	*He took the skin off an orange.*
Thug sí <u>d</u>'fhear an phoist é.	*She gave it to the postman.*

i

This preposition doesn't change nouns beginning with vowels, but becomes *in* in front of them.

> **Tá cónaí air i_n Éirinn.**   *He lives in Ireland.*
>
> **Tá sé ag stopadh i_n óstlann.**   *He is staying in a hotel.*

4 Simple prepositions and the singular article

- The singular article **an** often comes after a preposition and before a singular noun. It corresponds to *the* in English.

- The article is sometimes added to a preposition to make one word; sometimes it stays separate from the preposition and other times it completely changes the preposition. The table below shows each preposition with the article.

Preposition	Preposition with article
ag	*ag an*
ar	*ar an*
as	*as an*
chuig	*chuig an*
de	*den*
do	*don*
faoi	*faoin*
i	*sa/san* (**san** before vowels)
le	*leis an*
ó	*ón*
roimh	*roimh an*
thar	*thar an*
trí	*tríd an*
um	*um an*

- When a preposition is used with the article it often changes the noun that follows it.

- In Irish there are two ways in which nouns can be changed

when a preposition and an article come before them; we will
call these **Method 1** and **Method 2**. Nouns can either be eclipsed
or aspirated. It is useful to learn both.

4.1 Method 1

- This method mostly involves eclipsing the noun when this is
  possible. This method is used in every part of Ireland except
  Ulster.

- There are some prepositions which require aspiration all the
  time, as in Ulster.

- We can show the changes made to nouns by grouping the
  nouns according to the letter they begin with.

➤ *b-, c-, f-, g-, p-*

- Nouns beginning with these letters are eclipsed when there is a
  preposition and an article before them. The form of the
  preposition and article can be seen in the table above.

ag an _m_bainis	*at the wedding reception*
ar an _g_carr	*on the car*
leis an _bh_fear	*with the man*
faoin _n_grian	*under the sun*
ón _b_pobal	*from the community*

➤ *d-, l-, m-, n-, r-, s-, t-*

- Nouns beginning with these letters cannot be eclipsed and
  therefore stay the same.

leis an <u>d</u>líodóir	*with the lawyer*
roimh an <u>l</u>ón	*before lunch*
ar an <u>m</u>argadh	*on the market*
ón <u>n</u>éal	*from the cloud*
tríd an <u>r</u>é sin	*throughout that era*
ag an <u>s</u>coil	*at the school*
chuig an <u>t</u>each	*to the house*

➤ *a-/á-, e-/é-, i-/í-, o-/ó-, u-/ú-*

- Nouns beginning with these vowels cannot be eclipsed and therefore stay the same.

faoin <u>a</u>lt	*about the article*
san <u>e</u>aglais	*in the church*
leis an <u>i</u>m	*with the butter*
ag an <u>o</u>tharlann	*at the hospital*
chuig an <u>ú</u>darás	*to the authority*

- As mentioned above, there are a few prepositions that are not covered by these rules. The prepositions are **den, don, sa/san** (**san** with vowels and **f**).

➤ *b-, c-, f-, g-, m-, p-*

- Nouns beginning with these letters are aspirated when the above prepositions are used with the article.

den b<u>h</u>alla	*of the wall*
don c<u>h</u>at	*for the cat*

don fhreastalaí	*to the waiter*
sa ghairdín	*in the garden*
den mhullach	*off the top*
sa phost	*in the job*

➤ *d-, l-, n-, r-, t-*

- Nouns beginning with these letters cannot be aspirated and therefore stay the same.

den dochtúir	*of the doctor*
don leabharlann	*for the library*
sa nead	*in the nest*
den ridire	*of the knight*
don teach	*for the house*

➤ *a-/á-, e-/é-, i-/í-, o-/ó-, u-/ú-*

- Nouns beginning with these vowels cannot be aspirated and therefore stay the same. Notice that *san* is used instead of *sa*.

den alta	*of the nurse*
don eitleán	*for the plane*
san iasc	*on the fish*
den othar	*of the patient*
don údar	*for the author*

➤ *sn-, sl-, sr-, s-* +vowel

- *t-* is placed before **feminine** nouns beginning with these groups of letters.

don t͟slat	*for the rod*
sa t͟sraith	*in the series*
den t͟seachtain	*of the week*

- No change is made to **masculine** nouns beginning with these groups of letters.

den s͟neachta	*of the snow*
don s͟labhra	*for the chain*
sa s͟ruthán	*in the stream*
den s͟iopa	*of the shop*

4.2 Method 2

- This method is used in Ulster Irish and mostly involves aspiration.

- The prepositions **den, don, sa/san** (**san** with vowels) work the same way in this method as they do in **method 1**.

- We can show the changes made to nouns by grouping the nouns according to the letter they begin with.

➤ b-, c-, f-, g-, m-, p-

- Nouns beginning with these letters are aspirated.

ag an bhainis	*at the wedding reception*
ar an charr	*on the car*
leis an fhear	*with the man*
faoin ghrian	*under the sun*
den mhullach	*of the top*

ón p̲hobal	*from the community*

➤ **d-, l-, n-, r-, t-**

- Nouns beginning with these letters cannot be aspirated and therefore stay the same.

leis an d̲líodóir	*with the lawyer*
roimh an l̲ón	*before lunch*
ón n̲éal	*from the cloud*
tríd an r̲áithe	*through the quarter*
chuig an t̲each	*to the house*

➤ **a-/á-, e-/é-, i-/í-, o-/ó-, u-/ú-**

- Nouns beginning with these vowels cannot be eclipsed and therefore stay the same.

faoin a̲lt	*about the article*
san e̲aglais	*in the church*
leis an i̲m	*with the butter*
ag an o̲tharlann	*at the hospital*
chuig an ú̲darás	*to the authority*

➤ **sn-, sl-, sr-, s-** +vowel

- **t-** is placed before **feminine** nouns beginning with these groups of letters.

ar an t̲slat	*on the rod*
sa t̲sraith	*in the series*
tríd an t̲seachtain	*through the week*

No change is made to *masculine* nouns beginning with these groups of letters.

faoin ṣneachta	*under the snow*
ón ṣlabhra	*from the chain*
sa ṣruthán	*in the stream*
ag an ṣiopa	*at the shop*

i It is very common in Ulster to place *t-* before all nouns, both masculine and feminine after a preposition and an article but it is considered more correct to follow the pattern above.

5 Simple prepositions and the plural article

- The plural article *na* often comes after prepositions and before plural nouns. It corresponds to *the* in English.

- The table below shows each preposition with the article.

Preposition	Preposition with article
ag	*ag na*
ar	*ar na*
as	*as na*
chuig	*chuig ana*
de	*de na*
do	*do na*
faoi	*faoi na*
i	*sna*
le	*leis na*
ó	*ó na*
roimh	*roimh na*
thar	*thar na*
trí	*tríd na*
um	*um na*

- Nouns beginning with a consonant are not changed.

ag na ballaí	at the walls
ar na cannaí	on the cans
as na doirse	out of the doors
chuig na feirmeoirí	to the farmers

de na geataí	of the gates
faoi na línte	under the lines
sna monarchana	in the factories
leis na nóiméid	with the minutes
ó na póilíní	from the police
roimh na ranganna	before the classes
thar na seachtainí	over the weeks
tríd na tíortha	through the countries

- **h** is placed before nouns beginning with a vowel.

ag na haisteoirí	at the actors
ar na héin	on the birds
as na híomhánna	out of the images
chuig na húdair	to the authors
de na haistí	of the essays
do na heitleáin	for the planes
faoi na hinge	under the nails
sna hoícheanta	in the nights
leis na huiscí	with the waters
ó na haltraí	from the nurses
roimh na hÉireannaigh	before the Irishmen
thar na hinnill	over the engines
tríd na hothair	through the patients
um na huaireanta	about the hours

KEY POINTS

✔ Prepositions are words that come before nouns or pronouns and which link them to other words in a sentence.
✔ Prepositions can cause aspiration or eclipsis to the noun which follows.

RELATIVE CLAUSES

What is a relative clause?

We use relative clauses to give additional information about somebody or something without starting another sentence. For example, take the two sentences: *I saw a man. He was working here yesterday.* They could be combined into one sentence: *I saw the man who was working here yesterday.* The part of the sentence, *who was working here yesterday* is the relative clause.

In Irish, there are two types of relative clause, direct relative clauses and indirect relative clauses.

1 Direct relative clause

1.1 Overview

A direct relative clause is one in which the person or thing described in the clause is the subject or object of the verb:

*an cailín **a bhris** na rialacha*	*the girl <u>who broke</u> the rules*
*an gasúr **a thiocfaidh** anseo amárach*	*the boy <u>who will come</u> here tomorrow*
*an múinteoir **a theagascann** sa scoil*	*the teacher <u>who teaches</u> in the school*
*an teach **a cheannaigh mé***	*the house <u>which I bought</u>*
*an duine **a fheicim** gach maidin*	*the person <u>who I see</u> every morning*
*an t-airgead **a chaithfidh mé** ar saoire*	*the money <u>which I will spend</u> on holiday*

1.2 The direct relative particle *a*

A is used in all tenses with all verbs and aspirates the first consonant of all verbs, except in the following:

➤ With **tá**:

an fear <u>atá</u> anseo	*the man <u>who is</u> here*

➤ With the past tense of the verb **faigh** *get*:

an duine <u>a fuair</u> an duais	*the person <u>who got</u> the prize*

➤ All tenses of the verb **abair** *say*:

an bhean <u>a dúirt</u> sin	*the woman <u>who said</u> that*
an sagart <u>a déarfaidh</u> an t-aifreann	*the priest <u>who will say</u> the mass*

➤ The past autonomous of all verbs except **bhíothas, thángthas, chuathas, chualathas, chonacthas**:

Sin an fhuinneog <u>a briseadh.</u>	*That's the window <u>that was broken</u>.*
Chuala mé an t-amhrán <u>a ceoladh</u> ag mo bhainís.	*I heard the song <u>that was sung</u> at my wedding.*

➤ Verbs beginning with a **vowel** or **f** which have **d'** in front of them in the past tense or conditional:

an madra <u>a d'ól</u> an t-uisce	*the dog <u>that drank</u> the water*
Sin an déagóir <u>a d'fhágfadh</u> an teach láithreach dá mbeadh seans aige.	*That's the teenager <u>who would leave</u> the house immediately if he had the chance.*

1.3 Nach

The negative particle **nach** is used in **all** tenses with all verbs except in the past tense, when it is only used with the irregular verbs **bí** *be*, **déan** *do/make*, **faigh** *get*, **abair** *say*, **feic** *see*, **téigh** *go*. **Nach** eclipses and prefixes **n-** to verbs beginning with a vowel:

an múinteoir <u>nach dtagann</u> ar scoil gach lá	the teacher <u>who doesn't come</u> to school every day
an bhean <u>nach n-ólann</u> fíon	the woman <u>who doesn't drink</u> wine
an leanbh <u>nach bhfuair</u> an duais	the child <u>who didn't get</u> the prize

1.4 Nár

Nár is only used in the past tense with regular verbs and with the irregular verbs **beir** *grab*, **clois/cluin** *hear*, **ith** *eat*, **tabhair** *give*, **tar** *come*. **Nár** aspirates but has no effect on verbs beginning with vowels:

na scoláirí <u>nár bhris</u> na rialacha	the students <u>who didn't break</u> the rules
sin an buachaill <u>nár oscail</u> a bhronntanas	that's the boy <u>who didn't open</u> his present

1.5 Other uses of *a*

➤ After the interrogatives **cá mhéad** *how much*, **cá fhad** *how long*, **cathain** *when*, **cén uair** *when* and **conas** *how*, we use **a** in a similar way:

Cá mhéad duine a tháinig anseo aréir?	How many people came here last night?
Cá fhad a chaithfidh tú sa Fhrainc i mbliana?	How long will you spend in France this year?

Cathain a bheidh siad ar ais in Éirinn arís?	When will they be back in Ireland again?
Cén uair a chuala tú an scéal sin?	When did you hear that story?

➤ **a** is also used after **nuair** when and **mar** like:

<u>**Nuair a**</u> **bhaineann an Dún Craobh na hÉireann beidh mé sásta.**	When Down wins the All-Ireland I will be happy.
Bhí sé ina sheasamh ag an doras <u>**mar a**</u> **bheadh saighdiúir ann.**	He was standing at the door as though he were a soldier.

➤ After **cén uair?** when?, we always use **a**:

Cén uair a bheidh tú ann?	When will you be there?
Cén uair a rinne tú sin?	When did you do that?
Cén uair a rachaidh tú ar saoire?	When will you go on holidays?

2   Indirect relative clause

2.1   Overview

➤An indirect relative clause is one in which the person or thing
described in the clause is not the subject or object of the verb:

an fear <u>a bhfuil</u> a mhac tinn	*the man whose son is sick*
an bhean <u>a ndeachaigh</u> a mac abhaile go luath	*the woman whose son went home early*
an gluaisteán <u>a bhfuil</u> a úinéir taobh amuigh	*the car whose owner is outside*

➤**How to translate**: *with whom, to whom, in which, out of which, on which*

an múinteoir <u>a raibh</u> mé ag caint <u>leis</u>	*the teacher <u>with whom I was</u> talking/the teacher I was talking to*
an cófra <u>a bhfuil</u> na cupáin <u>ann</u>	*the cupboard <u>in which</u> the cups <u>are</u>/ the cupboard which the cups are in*
an seomra <u>a mbeidh</u> na páistí <u>ann</u>	*the room <u>in which</u> the children <u>will be</u>/ the room which the children will be in*
an duine <u>a dtugaim</u> cuidiú <u>dó</u>	*the person <u>to whom I give</u> help/ the person I give help to*

➤When the interrogatives *cé* who, *cad/céard* what are followed by a
preposition:

Cé leis a raibh tú ag caint?	*Who were you talking to? (With whom were you talking?)*
Cé dó a dtabharfaidh tú an t-airgead?	*Who will you give the money to? (To whom will you give the money?)*
Céard faoi a mbíonn siad ag gearán?	*What are they complaining about? (About what are they complaining?)*

➤ After the following phrases we use an indirect relative clause:

an áit/cén áit	the place/which place
an dóigh/cén dóigh	the way/which way
an fáth/cén fáth	the reason/what reason
cad chuige	why

Sin an áit a ndearna sé an damáiste.   *That is the place where he did the damage.*

Cén dóigh a ndéanann siad anseo é?   *What way is it done here?*

Cén fáth ar tháinig sé ar ais sa deireadh?   *Why did he come back in the end?*

2.2 The indirect relative particle *a*

➤ The indirect relative positive particle *a* is used in all tenses and eclipses the dependent form of the verb (the question form), except in the past tense when it is only used with with the irregular verbs **bí** *be*, **déan** *do/make*, **faigh** *get*, **abair** *say*, **feic** *see*, **téigh** *go*:

an bhean a raibh a mac anseo   *the woman whose son was here*

an fhoireann a mbainfidh a chaptaen imreoir na bliana   *the team whose captain will win player of the year*

an leabhar a mbeidh eagrán nua de ag teacht amach go luath   *the book which there will be a new version of out soon*

➤ The indirect negative particle *ar* is used in the past tense only and aspirates, except with the verbs mentioned in the section above. It aspirates and removes the *d'* from the verbs which begin with vowels in the past tense.

an gasúr _ar bhris a chara_ an fhuinneog	the boy _whose friend broke_ the window
an leabhar _ar bhain mé_ an clúdach _de_	the book _from which I removed_ the front cover
Sin an bhean _ar ól a cara_ do ghloine fíona.	That's the woman _whose friend drank_ your glass of wine.

2.3 Nach

Nach is used in all tenses with all verbs except in the past tense, when it is only used with the irregular verbs **bí** _be_, **déan** _do/make_, **faigh** _get_, **abair** _say_, **feic** _see_, **téigh** _go_. **Nach** eclipses and prefixes **n-** to verbs beginning with a vowel:

an múinteoir _nach dtagann_ a mhac ar scoil gach lá	the teacher _whose son doesn't come_ to school every day
an bhean _nach n-ólann_ a cara fíon	the woman _whose friend doesn't drink_ wine
an leanbh _nach bhfuair_ a athair an duais	the child _whose father didn't get_ the prize

2.4 The indirect relative negative particle _nár_

The indirect relative negative particle **nár** is only used in the past tense with regular verbs and with the irregular verbs **beir** _grab_, **clois/cluin** _hear_, **ith** _eat_, **tabhair** _give_, **tar** _come_. **Nár** aspirates but has no effect on verbs beginning with vowels:

na scoláirí _nár bhris a gcairde_ na rialacha	the students _whose friends didn't break_ the rules
sin an buachaill _nár oscail_ a athair a bhronntanas	that's the boy _whose father didn't open_ his present

> ## Típ
>
> We can use either direct or indirect relative clauses after the words
> **am** time, **lá** day, **oíche** night, **bliain** night or other nouns which imply
> time:
>
> | | |
> |---|---|
> | **Cén lá a bhí sé ann/** | *What day was he there?* |
> | **cén lá a raibh sé ann?** | |
> | **Cén bhliain a tharla sé/** | *What year did it happen?* |
> | **cén bhliain ar tharla sé?** | |

NUMBERS

There are four kinds of numbers in Irish:

Cardinal numbers 1: numbers which aren't followed by a noun – *one, two, three* etc

Cardinal numbers 2: numbers that are used directly with nouns – *one book, two pens, three cars* etc

Personal numbers: numbers that are used when talking about people – *duine, beirt, triúr, ceathrar* etc

Ordinal numbers: numbers which express the order in which things happen – *first, second* etc

1 Cardinal numbers 1

In basic counting, we must put *a* before the number with numbers 1–19.

1.1 Counting from 0–20

0	*náid*		
1	*a haon*	6	*a sé*
2	*a dó*	7	*a seacht*
3	*a trí*	8	*a hocht*
4	*a ceathair*	9	*a naoi*
5	*a cúig*	10	*a deich*

11	a haon déag	16	a sé déag
12	a dó dhéag	17	a seacht déag
13	a trí déag	18	a hocht déag
14	a ceathair déag	19	a naoi déag
15	a cúig déag	20	fiche

1.2 Counting above 20

21	fiche a haon	75	seachtó a cúig
22	fiche a dó	80	ochtó
23	fiche a trí	86	ochtó a sé
24	fiche a ceathair	90	nócha
25	fiche a cúig	97	nócha a seacht
26	fiche a sé	100	céad
27	fiche a seacht	120	céad a fiche
28	fiche a hocht	135	céad tríocha a cúig
29	fiche a naoi	200	dhá chéad
30	tríocha	300	trí chéad
31	tríocha a haon	400	ceithre chéad
40	daichead	500	cúig chéad
42	daichead a dó	600	sé chéad
50	caoga	700	seacht gcéad
53	caoga a trí	800	ocht gcéad
60	seasca	900	naoi gcéad
64	seasca a ceathair	1000	míle
70	seachtó	10, 000	deich míle

2 Cardinal numbers 2

In Irish some numbers change slightly when we place a noun after them. We also usually use the singular of the noun after numbers. The numbers 2 and 4 change to from *dó* to *dhá* (2) and from *ceathair* to *ceithre* (4) when we add nouns.

2.1 Counting nouns 1–6

- After the numbers 1–6, we **aspirate** nouns beginning with a consonant:

trí chupán	*three cups*
cúig thábla	*five tables*

- After the numbers 1–6, we do nothing to nouns beginning with a vowel:

dhá úll	*two apples*
sé uan	*six lambs*

cupán *cup*	**úll** *apple*
aon chupán amháin *one cup*	**aon úll amháin** *one apple*
dhá chupán *two cups*	**dhá úll** *two apples*
trí chupán *three cups*	**trí úll** *three apples*
ceithre chupán *four cups*	**ceithre úll** *four apples*
cúig chupán *five cups*	**cúig úll** *five apples*
sé chupán *six cups*	**sé úll** *six apples*

2.2 Counting nouns 7–10

After the numbers 7–10, we **eclipse** nouns beginning both with **consonants** and **vowels**:

seacht g̲cupán	*seven cups*
naoi d̲tábla	*nine tables*
ocht n̲-úll	*eight apples*
deich n̲-uan	*ten lambs*

cupán *cup*	**úll** *apple*
seacht g̲cupán *seven cups*	**seacht n-úll** *seven apples*
ocht g̲cupán *eight cups*	**ocht n-úll** *eight apples*
naoi g̲cupán *nine cups*	**naoi n-úll** *nine apples*
deich g̲cupán *ten cups*	**deich n-úll** *ten apples*

2.3 Counting nouns from 10–19

When counting from 10–19, we add **déag/dhéag** to the examples above. We add **dhéag** if the noun we are counting <u>ends</u> in a vowel.

trí chupán déag	*thirteen cups*
BUT	
trí chófra dh̲éag	*thirteen cupboards*
seacht n-úll déag	*seventeen apples*
BUT	
ocht n-oráiste dh̲éag	*eighteen oranges*

cupán *cup*	**cófra** *cupboard*	**úll** *apple*
aon c̲hupán déag *eleven cups*	**aon c̲hófra dhéag** *eleven cupboards*	**aon úll déag** *eleven apples*

dhá chupán déag *twelve cups*	**dhá chófra dhéag** *twelve cupboards*	**dhá úll déag** *twelve apples*
trí chupán déag *thirteen cups*	**trí chófra dhéag** *thirteen cupboards*	**trí úll déag** *thirteen apples*
ceithre chupán déag *fourteen cups*	**ceithre chófra dhéag** *fourteen cupboards*	**ceithre úll déag** *fourteen apples*
cúig chupán déag *fifteen cups*	**cúig chófra dhéag** *fifteen cupboards*	**cúig úll déag** *fifteen apples*
sé chupán déag *sixteen cups*	**sé chófra dhéag** *sixteen cupboards*	**sé úll déag** *sixteen apples*
seacht gcupán déag *seventeen cups*	**seacht gcófra dhéag** *seventeen cupboards*	**seacht n-úll déag** *seventeen apples*
ocht gcupán déag *eighteen cups*	**ocht gcófra dhéag** *eighteen cupboards*	**ocht n-úll déag** *eighteen apples*
naoi gcupán déag *nineteen cups*	**naoi gcófra dhéag** *nineteen cupboards*	**naoi n-úll déag** *nineteen apples*

2.4 Counting nouns above 20

When counting above 20, we add **fiche** 20, **tríocha** 30, **daichead** 40, etc to the examples above. When counting simply 20, 30, 40, etc, the noun is never changed.

cupán *cup*	**úll** *apple*
aon chupán is fiche *twenty-one cups*	**cúig úll is seasca** *sixty-five apples*
dhá chupán is tríocha *thirty-two cups*	**sé úll is seachtó** *seventy-six apples*
trí chupán is daichead *forty-three cups*	**seacht n-úll is ochtó** *eighty-seven apples*

ceithre chupán is caoga	*ocht n-úll is nócha*
fifty-four cups	*ninety-eight apples*

2.5 Counting nouns above 100

When counting above 100, we use the following system. We begin with the word for a hundred, followed by the smaller number, followed by the noun:

> **Céad** (*a hundred*) is **dhá mhíle** (and *two miles*)

céad peann/úll	*céad is dhá pheann/úll*
one hundred pens/apples	*one hundred and two pens/apples*
dhá chéad peann/úll	*dhá chéad is ocht bpeann/n-úll*
two hundred pens/apples	*two hundred and eight pens/apples*
trí chéad peann/úll	*seacht gcéad fiche is naoi bpeann/n-úll*
three hundred pens/apples	*seven hundred and twenty nine pens/ apples*
ceithre chéad peann/úll	*cúig chéad peann/úll*
four hundred pens/apples	*five hundred pens/apples*
sé chéad peann/úll	*seacht gcéad peann/úll*
six hundred pens/apples	*seven hundred pens/apples*
ocht gcéad pean n/úll	*naoi gcéad peann/úll*
eight hundred pens/apples	*nine hundred pens/apples*

2.6 Nouns with special forms after numbers

There are certain nouns which have a special form after numbers. These are:

> **bliain** *a year*; **ceann** *head/one*; **cloigeann** *head/one*;
> **seachtain** *week* and **uair** *hour/time*.

noun	after 2	after 3–6	after 7–10
bliain	dhá bhliain	trí-sé bliana	seacht-deich mbliana
ceann	dhá cheann	trí-sé cinn	seacht-deich gcinn
cloigeann	dhá chloigeann	trí-sé cloigne	seacht-deich gcloigne
seachtain	dhá sheachtain	trí-sé seachtaine	seacht-deich seachtaine
uair	dhá uair	trí-sé huaire	seacht-deich n-uaire

2.7 Money

➤The words for *euro* and *cent* stay the same no matter what number comes before:

euro/cent (amháin)	one euro/cent
dhá euro/cent	two euros/cents
trí euro/cent	three euros/cents
seacht euro/cent	seven euros/cents
ocht euro/cent	eight euros/cents

➤With Sterling, various changes occur:

punt agus pingin	pounds and pence

➤The rules for cardinal numbers 2 apply to **punt**:

punt (amháin)	one pound
dhá, trí, ceithre, cúig, sé phunt	two, three, four, five, six pounds
seacht, ocht, naoi, deich bpunt	seven, eight, nine, ten pounds

➤*Pingin*, however, has a special plural when used with numbers:

- **1–2**

pingin (amháin)	*one penny*
dhá phingin	*two pence*

- **3–10**

trí phingine	*three pence*
ceithre phingine	*four pence*
cúig phingine	*five pence*
sé phingine	*six pence*
seacht bpingine	*seven pence*
ocht bpingine	*eight pence*
naoi bpingine	*nine pence*
deich bpingine	*ten pence*

3   Personal numbers

3.1   Personal numbers 1–12

In Irish we have to use special forms for numbers when we are
counting people. These are:

Number	
1	**duine, duine amháin, aon duine amháin** *a person, a single person*
2	**beirt**
3	**triúr**
4	**ceathrar**
5	**cúigear**
6	**seisear**
7	**seachtar**
8	**ochtar**
9	**naonúr**
10	**deichniúr**
11	**(aon) duine dhéag**
12	**dáréag**

i When we use a noun after the personal numbers 2–10, we need a
special form of the plural called the genitive (see page 16).

beirt bhan	*two women*
triúr fear	*three men*
ceathrar múinteoirí	*four teachers*
cúigear amhránaithe	*five singers*

seisear gasúr	*six boys*
seachtar cailíní	*seven girls*
ochtar banaltraí	*eight nurses*
naonúr buachaillí	*nine boys*
deichniúr ban	*ten women*

> *Típ*
>
> The word **beirt** aspirates the noun which follows, except nouns
> that can't be aspirated and those that begin with **d**, **s** or **t**.
>
> | | |
> |---|---|
> | **beirt <u>ch</u>ailíní** | *two girls* |
> | BUT | |
> | **beirt daltaí** | *two students* |

3.2 Personal numbers above 12

When counting numbers of people above 12, we revert to the normal
counting system for nouns:

13	**trí ghasúr déag** *thirteen boys*
14	**ceithre dhuine dhéag** *fourteen people*
15	**cúig chailín déag** *fifteen girls*
16	**sé mhúinteoir déag** *sixteen teachers*
17	**seacht bpeileadóir déag** *seventeen footballers*
18	**ocht gcara dhéag** *eighteen friends*
19	**naoi bhfiaclóir déag** *nineteen dentists*
20	**fiche múinteoir** *twenty teachers*
30	**tríocha cara** *thirty friends*

40/50 etc	**daichead, caoga buachaill** forty/fifty boys
43	**trí chailín is daichead** forty–three girls
54	**ceithre phaisinéir is caoga** fifty–four passengers
65	**cúig phaisinéir is seasca** sixty–five passengers
98	**ocht bpaisinéir is nócha** ninety–eight passengers

4 Ordinal numbers

These are the numbers with which we describe the <u>order</u> in which things come.

In Irish, we usually place the article **an** in front of the ordinal number:

➤**chéad** *the first*

Típ

chéad aspirates the noun which follows if it begins with a consonant which can be aspirated. It has no effect on nouns which begin with vowels with **d, t** or **s**.

an chéad b<u>h</u>ean	*the first woman*
an chéad duais	*the first prize*
an chéad áit	*the first place*

➤ **the second – the tenth**

	bean *woman*	**áit** *place*
2nd	**an dara bean**	**an dara háit**
3rd	**an tríú bean**	**an tríú háit**
4th	**an ceathrú bean**	**an ceathrú háit**
5th	**an cúigiú bean**	**an cúigiú háit**
6th	**an séú bean**	**an séú háit**
7th	**an seachtú bean**	**an seachtú háit**
8th	**an t-ochtú bean**	**an t-ochtú háit**

9th	an naoú bean	an naoú háit
10th	an deichiú bean	an deichiú háit
11th	an t-aonú bean déag	an t-aonú háit déag
12th	an darabean déag	an dara háit déag
13th – 19th	an tríú bean déag – an naoú bean déag	an tríú háit déag – an naoú háit déag
20th – 90th	an fichiú, an tríochadú, an daicheadú, an caogadú, an seascadú, an seachtódú, an t-ochtódú, an nóchadú bean	an fichiú, an tríochadú, an daicheadú, an caogadú, an seascadú, an seachtódú, an t-ochtódú, an nóchadú háit
21st	an t-aonú bean is fiche	an t-aonú háit is fiche
32nd	an dara bean is tríocha	an dara háit is tríocha
45th	an séú bean is daichead	an séú háit is daichead
100th	an céadú bean	an céadú háit
1000th	an míliú bean	an míliú háit

TIME AND DATE

1   Time

ℹ️ To ask the time, we say **Cén t-am é?** *What time is it?*

➤If we wish to tell the time, we use the **cardinal numbers**.

Tá sé a haon a chlog.	*It is one o'clock.*
Tá sé a dó a chlog.	*It is two o'clock.*

⇨ For more information on the cardinal numbers, see chapter 15.

Tá sé It is ...	**cúig go dtí a haon/a dó/etc**	*five to one/two/etc*
	deich go dtí a haon/a dó/etc	*ten to one/two/etc*
	ceathrú go dtí a haon/a dó/etc	*quarter to one/two/etc*
	fiche go dtí a haon/a dó/etc	*twenty to one/two/etc*
	fiche a cúig go dtí a haon/a dó/etc	*twenty-five to one/two/etc*

Tá sé It is ...	**cúig i ndiaidh a haon/a dó/etc**	*five past one/two/etc*
	deich i ndiaidh a haon/a dó/etc	*ten past one/two/etc*
	ceathrú i ndiaidh a haon/a dó/etc	*a quarter past one/two/etc*
	fiche i ndiaidh a haon/a dó/etc	*twenty past one/two/etc*
	fiche a cúig i ndiaidh a haon/a dó/etc	*twenty-five past one/two/etc*

➤If we want to say *It is three minutes past ten*, we say:

Tá sé trí nóiméad i ndiaidh a deich.

or if we want to say *It is twenty eight minutes to twelve*, we say:

Tá sé ocht nóiméad is fiche go dtí a dó dhéag.

☑ The Irish word for *midnight* is **meánoíche**, and *midday* is **meánlae**.

KEY POINTS

> ✔ We use the cardinal numbers to tell the time.
> ✔ *i ndiaidh* means *past* and *go dtí* means *to*.
> ✔ *ceathrú* means *quarter* and **leath** means *half*.

2   Days of the week

The days of the week appear in two forms in Irish, with either the article **an** or the word **Dé** preceding them.

➤ The article **an** is used when simply listing days: **an Luan** Monday, **an Mháirt** Tuesday

ar an Chéadaoin	on a Wednesday, on Wednesdays
Inniu an Chéadaoin.	Today is Wednesday.
an Chéadaoin ina dhiaidh sin	the following Wednesday

➤ The word **Dé** is used when referring to (on) a specific day of the week:

Dé Luain seo chugainn	next Monday
tráthnóna Dé Céadaoin	on Wednesday evening
Oíche Dé Máirt	on Tuesday night

an Luan Monday	**Dé Luain** on Monday
an Mháirt Tuesday	**Dé Máirt** on Tuesday
an Chéadaoin Wednesday	**Dé Céadaoin** on Wednesday
an Déardaoin Thursday	**Déardaoin** on Thursday
an Aoine Friday	**Dé hAoine** on Friday
an Satharn Saturday	**Dé Sathairn** on Saturday
an Domhnach Sunday	**Dé Domhnaigh** on Sunday

ⓘ The spelling of the days is different if preceded by **Dé**.

KEY POINTS

✔ When we are simply listing the days, we place *an* in front of the day in question.

✔ When we are talking about **on** a specific day, we place *Dé* in front of the day in question.

3 Dates

➤When we are simply listing the months, we use the following:

Eanáir	January
Feabhra	February
Márta	March
Aibreán	April
Bealtaine	May
Meitheamh	June
Iúil	July
Lúnasa	August
Meán Fómhair	September
Deireadh Fómhair	October
Samhain	November
Nollaig	December

🛈 To ask what the date is we say:

Cén dáta atá ann inniu?   What is the date today?

➤To say what the date is, we use the **ordinal numbers**, and the following structure:

Inniu (today) **+ day + de mhí** + month

🛈 The spelling of the month changes slightly after **de mhí**.

Inniu an chéad lá de mhí Eanáir. Today is the first of January.

⇨ For more information on the cardinal numbers, see chapter 15.

Date

an chéad lá	the first (day)
an dara lá	the second (day)
an tríú lá	the third (day)
an ceathrú lá	the fourth (day)
an cúigiú lá	the fifth (day)
an séú lá	the sixth (day)
an seachtú lá	the seventh (day)
an t-ochtú lá	the eighth (day)
an naoú lá	the ninth (day)
an deichiú lá	the tenth (day)
an t-aonú lá déag	the eleventh (day)
an dara lá déag	the twelfth (day)
an tríú lá déag	the thirteenth (day)
an ceathrú lá déag	the fourteenth (day)
an cúigiú lá déag	the fifteenth (day)
an séú lá déag	the sixteenth (day)
an seachtú lá déag	the seventeenth (day)
an t-ochtú lá déag	the eighteenth (day)
an naoú lá déag	the nineteenth (day)
an fichiú lá	the twentieth (day)
an t-aonú lá is fiche	the twenty-first (day)
an dara lá is fiche	the twenty-second (day)
an tríú lá is fiche	the twenty-third (day)
an ceathrú lá is fiche	the twenty-fourth (day)
an cúigiú lá is fiche	the twenty-fifth (day)
an séú lá is fiche	the twenty-sixth (day)

an seachtú lá is fiche	the twenty-seventh (day)
an t-ochtú lá is fiche	the twenty-eighth (day)
an naoú lá is fiche	the twenty-ninth (day)
an tríochadú lá	the thirtieth (day)
an t-aonú lá is tríocha	the thirty-first (day)

Month	
de mhí Eanáir	of January
de mhí Feabhra	of February
de mhí an Mhárta	of March
de mhí Aibreáin	of April
de mhí na Bealtaine	of May
de mhí an Mheithimh	of June
de mhí Iúil	of July
de mhí Lúnasa	of August
de mhí Mheán Fómhair	of September
de mhí Dheireadh Fómhair	of October
de mhí na Samhna	of November
de mhí na Nollag	of December

KEY POINTS

✔ When we are saying what the date is, we use the **ordinal numbers.**
✔ We also must use a special form of the months when saying what date it is.

NAMES AND SURNAMES

1   Names

> Names in Irish are either masculine or feminine and have common, vocative and genitive forms. The personal names of men are masculine, those of women feminine.

1.1   Names of men

There are three types of men's names:

1. Those that end in a **broad consonant**
   (a consonant preceded by *a, o, u*)
2. Those that end in a **vowel** or **slender consonant**
   (a consonant preceded by *i, e*)
3. A small number of other masculine names.

➤Names that end in a **broad consonant**

The main changes which occur are underlined. These are aspiration and slenderizing (placing the letter *i* before the last letter of the word).

Examples:
Breandán, Cathal, Ciarán, Colmán, Dónall, Lorcán, Peadar, Pól

Normal	Breandán	Cathal	Dónall
Vocative	A B<u>h</u>reandá<u>i</u>n, cá bhfuil tú? *Breandán, where are you?*	A C<u>h</u>atha<u>i</u>l, bí ciúin! *Cathal, be quiet!*	A D<u>h</u>óna<u>i</u>ll, ith do dhinnéar! *Dónall, eat your dinner!*

Genitive	*teach Bhreandáin* Breandán's house	*teach Chathail* Cathal's house	*teach Dhónaill* Dónall's house

➤ Names that end in a **vowel** or **slender consonant**

The main changes that occur are underlined. This is usually aspiration.

Examples: *Eoin, Pádraig, Ruairí*

Normal	Eoin	Pádraig	Ruairí
Vocative	*A Eoin, cá bhfuil tú?* Eoin, where are you?	*A Phádraig, bí ciúin!* Pádraig, be quiet!	*A Ruairí, ith do dhinnéar!* Ruairí, eat your dinner!
Genitive	*teach Eoin* Eoin's house	*teach Phádraig* Pádraig's house	*teach Ruairí* Ruairí's house

➤ Other masculine names

The changes can vary, and it is worth learning them individually.

Examples: *Críostóir, Diarmaid, Aonghas*

Normal	Críostóir	Diarmaid	Aonghas
Vocative	*A Chríostóir, cá bhfuil tú?* Críostóir, where are you?	*A Dhiarmaid, bí ciúin!* Diarmaid, be quiet!	*A Aonghais, ith do dhinnéar* Aonghas, eat your dinner!
Genitive	*teach Chríostóra* Críostóir's house	*teach Phádraig* Pádraig's house	*teach Ruairí* Ruairí's house

1.2 Names of women

These are much easier to deal with, and apart from very few exceptions, the only change which occurs is aspiration.

Examples: *Áine, Eithne, Gráinne, Máire, Máirín, Róisín, Sinéad*

Normal	*Áine*	*Eithne*	*Sinéad*
Vocative	*A Áine, cá bhfuil tú?* *Áine, where are you?*	*A Eithne, bí ciúin!* *Eithne, be quiet!*	*A Shinéad, ith do dhinnéar!* *Sinéad, eat your dinner!*
Genitive	*teach Áine* *Áine's house*	*teach Eithne* *Eithne's house*	*teach Shinéad* *Sinéad's house*

KEY POINTS

✔ There are three main types of masculine names in Irish.
✔ The spelling of masculine names can change by aspiration and by slenderizing.
✔ Feminine names are usually only aspirated.

2 Surnames

A lot of surnames found in Ireland have O' or Mc/Mac in front of them. These are anglicised versions of **Ó** (*descendant of*) and **Mac** (*son of*). The Irish versions of surnames, however, have masculine, feminine, vocative and genitive forms.

2.1 Ó surnames

➤Ó surnames followed by consonants that can be aspirated:

	Masculine	**Feminine**
Normal Form	*Tomás Ó Ciaráin*	*Máire Ní Chiaráin*
Vocative	*A Thomáis Uí Chiaráin, tar anseo!* Tomás Ó Ciaráin, come here!	*A Mháire Ní Chiaráin, fan mar a bhfuil tú!* Máire Ní Chiaráin, stay where you are!
Genitive	*teach Thomáis Uí Chiaráin* Tomás Ó Ciaráin's house	*teach Mháire Ní Chiaráin* Máire Ní Chiaráin's house

➤Ó surnames followed by consonants which can't be aspirated:

	Masculine	**Feminine**
Normal Form	*Peadar Ó Neachtain*	*Connlaith Ní Laoire*
Vocative	*A Pheadair Uí Neachtain, seas amach!* Peadar Ó Neachtain, stand out!	*A Chonnlaith Ní Laoire, cá bhfuil do chóta!* Connlaith Ní Laoire, where is your coat?

Genitive	**teach Pheadair <u>Uí</u> Neachtain** *Peadar Ó Neachtain's house*	**teach Chonnlaith Ní Laoire** *Connlaith Ní Laoire's house*

➤**Ó** surnames followed by vowels:

	Masculine	**Feminine**
Normal Form	**Micheál Ó <u>h</u>Aodha**	**Cáitlín Ní Aodha**
Vocative	**A Mhicheáil <u>Uí</u> Aodha, bí ciúin!** *Micheál Ó hAodha, be quiet!*	**A Cháitlín Ní Aodha, bíodh múineadh ort!** *Cáitlín Ní Aodha, have some manners!*
Genitive	**teach Mhicheáil <u>Uí</u> Aodha** *Micheál Ó hAodha's house*	**teach Cháitlín Ní Aodha** *Cáitlín Ní Aodha's house*

2.2 *Mac* surnames

➤*Mac* surnames followed by consonants that can be aspirated:

	Masculine	**Feminine**
Normal Form	**Séamus Mac Mathúna**	**Sorcha Nic Mhathúna**
Vocative	**A Shéamuis <u>Mhic</u> M<u>h</u>athúna, suigh síos!** *Séamus Mac Mathúna, sit down!*	**A Shorcha Nic M<u>h</u>athúna, cad é a rinne tú?** *Sorcha Nic Mathúna, what have you done?*
Genitive	**teach Shéamuis <u>Mhic</u> M<u>h</u>athúna** *Séamus Mac Mathúna's house*	**teach Shorcha Nic M<u>h</u>athúna** *Sorcha Nic Mhathúna's house*

➤ *Mac* surnames followed by consonants which can't be aspirated include surnames beginning with the letter *c*, even though this letter can usually be aspirated.

	Masculine	Feminine
Normal Form	*Peadar Mac Coinnigh*	*Nóirín Nic Coinnigh*
Vocative	*A Pheadair Mhic Cionnaigh, ná déan sin!* Peadar Mac Coinnigh, don't do that!	*A Nóirín Nic Coinnigh, cá bhfuil tú?* Nóirín Nic Coinnigh, where are you?
Genitive	*teach Pheadair <u>Mhic Cionnaigh</u>* Peadar Mac Coinnigh's house	*teach Nóirín Nic Coinnigh* Nóirín Nic Coinnigh's house

➤ *Mac* surnames followed by vowels:

	Masculine	Feminine
Normal Form	*Marcas Mac Oscair*	*Síle Nic Oscair*
Vocative	*A Mharcais <u>Mhic</u> Oscair, cuidigh liom!* Marcus Mac Oscair, help me!	*A Shíle Nic Oscair, cuir ort do chóta!* Síle Nic Oscair, put on your coat!
Genitive	*teach Mharcais <u>Mhic</u> Oscair* Marcas Mac Oscar's house	*teach Shíle Nic Oscair* Síle Nic Oscar's house

2.3 *Ó* and *Mac* as surnames by marriage

➤If a woman marries a man with an **Ó** surname, **Ó** changes to **Uí**:
So, if **Connlaith Ní Laoire** marries **Seán Ó Briain**, her name changes to
Connlaith Uí Bhriain, literally meaning **Ó Briain's Connlaith**!

➤If a woman marries a man with a **Mac** surname, **Mac** changes to
Mhic: So, if **Sorcha Nic Mhathúna** marries **Marcas Mac Oscair**, her
name changes to **Sorcha Mhic Oscair**, literally meaning **Mac Oscair's
Sorcha**!

KEY POINTS

✔ **Ó** changes to **Ní** when the surname is feminine.
✔ **Ó** changes to **Uí** in the vocative and genitive cases.
✔ **Mac** changes to **Nic** when the surname is feminine.
✔ **Mac** changes to **Mhic** in the vocative and genitive cases.

PLACE NAMES

The vast majority of place names in Ireland come from the original Irish but now appear largely in their Anglicized forms. Like most other nouns, place names have different forms, depending on their case.

➤Ireland

There is sometimes confusion about the different versions of the Irish name for Ireland. Basically, there are three forms regularly seen:

- the normal form: *Éire*

    Tá Éire chun tosaigh sa chluiche.   *Ireland is ahead in the game.*

    Tá Éire ag imirt go maith inniu.   *Ireland is playing well today.*

- the dative: *Éirinn*

    Bhí mé in Éirinn i rith an tsamhraidh.   *I was in Ireland during the summer.*

- the genitive: *Éireann*

    Tá muintir na hÉireann iontach cairdiúil.   *Irish people are very friendly.*

➤The provinces of Ireland

There are four provinces in Ireland and their names have distinctive

forms in the genitive. They also have adjectives associated with them
to describe people from that province:

	Normal Form	Genitive	Adjective
Ulster	**Ulaidh**	**Cúige Uladh** *the province of Ulster*	**Ultach** *a person from Ulster*
Leinster	**Laighin**	**Cúige Laighean** *the province of Leinster*	**Laighneach** *a person from Leinster*
Munster	**Mumhain**	**Cúige Mumhan** *the province of Munster*	**Muimhneach** *a person from Munster*
Connaught	**Connachta**	**Cúige Chonnacht** *the province of Connaught*	**Connachtach** *a person from Connaught*

➤Counties

There are thirty-two counties in Ireland, each of which has a normal
form and a genitive form. To highlight this the following table shows
the genitive form after the word ***contae*** *county*.

	County	Genitive
Ulster	**Aontroim** *Antrim* **Ard Mhacha** *Armagh* **an Cabhán** *Cavan* **Doire** *Derry* **An Dún** *Down* **Dún na nGall/Tír Chonaill** *Donegal* **Fear Manach** *Fermanagh* **Muineachán** *Monaghan* **Tír Eoghain** *Tyrone*	**Contae Aontroma** **Contae Ard Mhacha** **Contae an Chabháin** **Contae Dhoire** **Contae an Dúin** **Contae Dhún na nGall/ Contae Thír Chonaill** **Contae Fhear Manach** **Contae Mhuineacháin** **Contae Thír Eoghain**

Leinster	**Baile Átha Cliath** *Dublin*	*Contae Bhaile Átha Cliath*
	Ceatharlach *Carlow*	*Contae Cheatharlach*
	Cill Dara *Kildare*	*Contae Chill Dara*
	Cill Mhantáin *Wicklow*	*Contae Chill Mhantáin*
	an Iarmhí *Westmeath*	*Contae na hIarmhí*
	Laois *Laois*	*Contae Laoise*
	Loch Garman *Wexford*	*Contae Loch Garman*
	Longfort *Longfort*	*Contae Longfoirt*
	Lú *Louth*	*Contae Lú*
	an Mhí *Meath*	*Contae na Mí*
	Uíbh Fhailí *Offaly*	*Contae Uíbh Fhailí*
Connaught	**Gaillimh** *Galway*	*Contae na Gaillimhe*
	Liatroim *Leitrim*	*Contae Liatroma*
	Maigh Eo *Mayo*	*Contae Mhaigh Eo*
	Ros Comáin *Roscommon*	*Contae Ros Comáin*
	Sligeach *Sligo*	*Contae Shligigh*
Munster	**Ciarraí** *Kerry*	*Contae Chiarraí*
	an Clár *Clare*	*Contae an Chláir*
	Corcaigh *Cork*	*Contae Chorcaí*
	Luimneach *Limerick*	*Contae Luimnigh*
	Port Láirge *Waterford*	*Contae Phort Láirge*
	Tiobráid Árann *Tipperary*	*Contae Thiobráid Árann*

➤ The article with place names

A lot of place names in Irish, whether they are towns, cities or even rivers, can be preceded by the definite article **an**, even though *the* does not appear in the Anglicised version.

An tIúr	*Newry*
An Ómaigh	*Omagh*
An Bhóinn	*River Boyne*
An Longfort	*Longfort*

➤**Adjectives and nouns from place names**

Often adjectives and nouns which describe nationality or relationships with provinces or towns are formed from place names.

Country/County	Adjective/Noun
An Fhrainc France	**Francach** French/French person
Sasana England	**Sasanach** English/English person
An Ghearmáin Germany	**Gearmánach** German/German person
Tír Chonaill Donegal	**Conallach** Donegal person
An Eoraip Europe	**Eorpach** European/European person

➤**Place names in the genitive**

If the article comes before the place name, then we apply the same rules as we would to a definite noun in the genitive case.

Place name	Genitive
an Teampall Mór Templemore	**muintir an Teampaill Mhóir** the people of Templemore
an Mullach Bán Mullaghbawn	**peileadóirí an Mhullaigh Bháin** the Mullaghbawn footballers

⇨   See section 3.3 of chapter 2 on the genitive

PREFIXES AND SUFFIXES

What are prefixes and suffixes?
A prefix is a group of letters added to the beginning of a word to alter its meaning, whilst a suffix is a group of letters added to the end of a word to alter its meaning.

1 Prefixes

➤A hyphen is never written between prefixes and the beginning of the word unless it is between two vowels:

ró-ard	*too tall*
BUT	
róbheag	*too small*

or after **an-** (which is a prefix which intensifies meaning)

an-chiúin	*very quiet*

or after **dea-**

dea-dhuine	*a nice person*

➤Some prefixes cause aspiration to the beginning of the following word:

cliste	*intelligent* but
cárchliste	*extremely intelligent*

➤At times we can't translate the examples with the exact meaning of the prefix. For example, the prefix **dian** *(intense)*, can be used in **dianghrá** as the word for *true love*.

Prefix	Meaning	Examples
an-	very	**an-bheag** *very small* **an-mhór** *very big* **an-láidir** *very strong* **an-lá** *a great day* **an-cheo** *very thick fog*
ard	high/main	**ardchaighdeán** *high standard* **ardmhéara** *lord mayor* **ardmheas** *great respect, esteem* **ardoifig** *head office*
dian	intense	**dianghrá** *intense love* **dianobair** *intense work* **dianmhaith** *very good* **dianchúrsa** *a crash course*
fíor	true/extremely	**fíorchinnte** *absolutely sure* **fíorbheagán** *extremely little* **fíordheas** *extremely nice* **fíormhaith** *extremely good*
lán	full/totally	**lánbhuíoch** *very thankful* **lánsásta** *totally happy* **lántoilteanach** *fully willing*
ró	too	**ró-ard** *too hard* **róbheag** *too small* **ró-íseal** *too low* **rómhór** *too big*
sár	extremely	**sárchliste** *extremely intelligent* **sármhaith** *extremely good* **sár-oilte** *extremely well educated*
mí	un-/in (makes the meaning opposite)	**míbhéasach** *unmannerly* **mícheart** *incorrect* **mí-ámharach** *unlucky*

neamh	un-/in/ir (makes the meaning opposite)	**neamhchoitianta** *uncommon* **neamhghnách** *unusual* **neamhrialta** *irregular* **neamhbheo** *dead (unliving)*
ais	*re-*	**aisíoc** *repay* **aiséirí** *resurrection*
dea-	*nice/good*	**dea-ainm** *good name* **dea-bhéasach** *well mannered* **dea-dhuine** *a good person* **dea-thoil** *good will*
meán	*middle/medium*	**meánaosta** *middle aged* **meánscoil** *secondary (middle) school* **meánlae** *midday* **meánoíche** *midnight*
príomh	*main*	**príomhchathair** *capital (main) city* **príomhoide** *headmaster* **príomhdhoras** *main door*
réamh	*before*	**réamhobair** *preparatory work* **réamhthaispeántas** *preview* **réamhaisnéis** *forecast*
síor	*eternal/ constant*	**síorbháisteach** *constant rain* **síorchaint** *constant talk* **síorchaoineadh** *constant crying*

2 Suffixes

➤The following are diminutive suffixes, i.e, they make the word to which they are added small: **-án, -ín, -óg**.

Suffix	Examples		
-án	**bóthan** *a small hut*	**cnocán** *a hillock*	**sruthán** *a small stream*
-ín	**capaillín** *a small horse*	**asailín** *a small donkey*	**teachín** *a cottage*
-óg	**bábóg** *a doll*	**míoltóg** *a midge*	**síóg** *a fairy*

➤The suffixes **-aire, -amh, -í, -éir, -óir** and **-úir** are used for professions or for someone who carries out an action on a regular basis, like the suffix *-er* in English in teach<u>er</u>.

Suffix	Examples		
-aire	**iascaire** *a fisherman*	**píobaire** *a piper*	**teachtaire** *a messenger*
-amh	**breitheamh** *a judge*	**ollamh** *professor*	
-í	**gréasaí** *a shoemaker*	**seanchaí** *a storyteller*	**tiománaí** *a driver*
-éir	**búistéir** *a butcher*	**siúinéir** *a joiner*	
-óir	**bádóir** *a boatman*	**ceoltóir** *a musician*	**múinteoir** *a teacher*
-úir	**dochtúir** *a doctor*	**saighdiúir** *a soldier*	**táilliúir** *a tailor*

➤We also can attach suffixes to nouns to create adjectives. These suffixes are **-ach, -da, -ga, -mhar, -ta** and **-lann**.

Suffix	Examples			
-ach	cnocach hilly	feargach angry	gnóthach busy	Gaelach Irish
-da	Gallda foreign	rúnda secretive	seanda ancient	
-ga	beoga lively	diaga divine	ríoga royal	
-mhar	bríomhar lively	ciallmhar sensible	glórmhar glorious	
-ta	faiseanta fashionable	náisiúnta national		
-ach (with person)	Albanach Scottish	Francach French	Sasanach English	
-lann (a place)	amharclann theatre	leabharlann library		

KEY POINTS

✔ Prefixes are added to the beginning of a word and change its meaning.
✔ Prefixes can sometimes aspirate.
✔ Suffixes come at the end of a word.

MAIN INDEX

VERB TABLES

INTRODUCTION

The **Verb Tables** in the following section contain 26 tables of Irish verbs (11 irregular and 15 regular) in alphabetical order. Each table shows you the following forms: **Present, Past, Future, Present subjunctive, Conditional, Imperative** and the **Verbal noun** and **Verbal adjective**. For more information on these tenses, how they are formed, when they are used and so on, you should look at the section on **Verbs** in the main text.

The **Verb Index** at the end of this section contains over 500 verbs, each of which is cross-referred to one of the verbs given in the Verb Tables. The table shows the patterns that the verb listed in the index follows.

1 **abair** (to say, sing)

PRESENT
deirim
deir tú
deir sé
deir sí
deirimid
deir sibh
deir said

deirtear*

PRESENT SUBJUNCTIVE
deire mé
deire tú
deire sé
deire sí
deirimid
deire sibh
deire siad

deirtear*

PAST
dúirt mé
dúirt tú
dúirt sé
dúirt sí
dúramar
dúirt sibh
dúirt said

dúradh*

IMPERATIVE
abraim
abair
abradh sé
abradh sí
abraimis
abraigí
abraidís

deirtear*

FUTURE
déarfaidh mé
déarfaidh tú
déarfaidh sé
déarfaidh sí
déarfaimid
déarfaidh sibh
déarfaidh said

déarfar*

CONDITIONAL
déarfainn
déarfá
déarfadh sé
déarfadh sí
déarfaimis
déarfadh sibh
déarfaidís

déarfaí*

VERBAL NOUN
rá

VERBAL ADJECTIVE
ráite

2 beir (to give birth to, lay *etc*)

PRESENT

beirim
beireann tú
beireann sé
beireann sí
beirimid
beireann sibh
beireann said

beirtear*

PRESENT SUBJUNCTIVE

beire mé
beire tú
beire sé
beire sí
beirimid
beire sibh
beire siad

beirtear*

PAST

rug mé
rug tú
rug sé
rug sí
rugamar
rug sibh
rug said

rugadhr*

IMPERATIVE

beirim
beir
beireadh sé
beireadh sí
beirimis
beirigí
bheiridís

beirtear*

FUTURE

béarfaidh mé
béarfaidh tú
béarfaidh sé
béarfaidh sí
béarfaimid
béarfaidh sibh
béarfaidh said

béarfar*

CONDITIONAL

bhéarfainn
bhéarfá
bhéarfadh sé
bhéarfadh sí
bhéarfaimis
bhéarfadh sibh
bhéarfaidís

bhéarfaí*

VERBAL NOUN

breith

VERBAL ADJECTIVE

beirthe

* autonomous form

3 bí (to be)

PRESENT (INDEPENDENT)

táim (tá mé)
tá tú
tá sé
tá sí
táimid
tá sibh
tá said

táthar*

PRESENT (HABITUAL)

bím
bíonn tú
bíonn sé
bíonn sí
bímid
bíonn sibh
bíonn siad

bítear*

PRESENT (DEPENDENT)

nílim (níl mé), go bhfuil mé
níl tú, go bhfuil tú
níl sé, go bhfuil sé
níl sí, go bhfuil sí
nílimid, go bhfuilimid
níl sibh, go bhfuil sibh
níl said, go bhfuil said

níltear*

go bhfuiltear*

PAST (INDEPENDENT)

bhí mé
bhí tú
bhí sé
bhí sí
bhíomar
bhí sibh
bhí siad

bhíothas*

PAST (DEPENDENT)

raibh mé
raibh tú
raibh sé
raibh sí
rabhamar
raibh sibh
raibh said

rhabthas*

FUTURE

beidh mé
beidh tú
beidh sé
beidh sí
beimid
beidh sibh
beidh siad

beifear*

CONDITIONAL

bheinn
bheifeá
bheadh sé
bheadh sí
bheimis
bheadh sibh
bheidis

bheifí*

IMPERATIVE

bím
bí
bíodh sé
bíodh sí
bímis
bígí
bídís

bítear*

VERBAL NOUN

bheith

VERBAL OF NECESSITY

beite

* autonomous form

4

4 **déan** (to do, make)

PRESENT

déanaim
déanann tú
déanann sé
déanann sí
déanaimid
déanann sibh
déanann said

déantar*

PRESENT SUBJUNCTIVE

déana mé
déana tú
déana sé
déana sí
déanaimid
déana sibh
déana siad

déantar*

PAST (INDEPENDENT)

rinne mé
rinne tú
rinne sé
rinne sí
rinneamar
rinne sibh
rinne said

rinneadh*

IMPERATIVE

déanaim
déan
déanadh sé
déanadh sí
déanaimis
déanaigí
déanaidís

déantar*

PAST (DEPENDENT)

ní dhearna mé	ní dhearnamar
go ndearna mé	go ndearnamar
ní dhearna tú	ní dhearna sibh
go ndearna tú	go ndearna sibh
ní dhearna sé	ní dhearna said
go ndearna sé	go ndearna siad
ní dhearna sí	
go ndearna si	
ní dhearnadh*	go ndearnadh*

FUTURE

déanfaidh mé
déanfaidh tú
déanfaidh sé
déanfaidh sí
déanfaimid
déanfaidh sibh
déanfaidh siad

déanfar*

CONDITIONAL

dhéanfainn
dhéanfá
dhéanfadh sé
dhéanfadh sí
dhéanfaimis
dhéanfadh sibh
dhéanfaidís

dhéanfaí*

VERBAL NOUN

déanamh

VERBAL ADJECTIVE

déanta

* autonomous form

5 **faigh** (to get, find, *etc*)

PRESENT	PRESENT SUBJUNCTIVE
faighim	faighe mé
faigheann tú	faighe tú
faigheann sé	faighe sé
faigheann sí	faighe sí
faighimid	faighimid
faigheann sibh	faighe sibh
faigheann said	faighe siad
faightear*	faightear*

PAST	IMPERATIVE
fuair mé	faighim
fuair tú	faigh
fuair sé	faigheadh sé
fuair sí	faigheadh sí
fuaireamar	faighimis
fuair sibh	faighigí
fuair said	faighidís
fuarthas*	faightear*

FUTURE (INDEPENDENT)	CONDITIONAL (INDEPENDENT)
gheobhaidh mé	gheobhainn
gheobhaidh tú	gheofá
gheobhaidh sé	gheobhadh sé
gheobhaidh sí	gheobhadh sí
gheobhaimid	gheobhaimis
gheobhaidh said	gheobhadh sibh
gheobhaidh said	gheobhaidís
gheofar*	gheofaí

FUTURE (DEPENDENT)	CONDITIONAL (DEPENDENT)
ní bhfaighidh mé	ní bhfaighinn
ní bhfaighidh tú	ní bhfaighfeá
ní bhfaighidh sé	ní bhfaigheadh sé
ni bhfaighidh sí	ní bhfaigheadh sí
ní bhfaighimid	ní bhfaighimis
ní bhfaighidh sibh	ní bhfaigheadh sibh
ní bhfaighidh said	ní bhfaighidís
ní bhfaighfear*	ní bhfaighfí*

VERBAL NOUN	VERBAL ADJECTIVE
fáil	faighte

6 **feic** (to see, seem)

PRESENT

feicim
feiceann tú
feiceann sé
feiceann sí
feicimid
feiceann sibh
feiceann said

feictear*

PRESENT SUBJUNCTIVE

feice mé
feice tú
feice sé
feice sí
feicimid
feice sibh
feice siad

feictear*

PAST (INDEPENDENT)

chonaic mé
chonaic tú
chonaic sé
chonaic sí
chonaiceamar
chonaic sibh
chonaic said

chonacthas*

IMPERATIVE

feicim
feic
feiceadh sé
feiceadh sí
feicimis
feicigí
feicidís

PAST (DEPENDENT)

ní fhaca mé
ní fhaca tú
ní fhaca sé
ní fhaca sí
ní fhacamar
ní fhaca sibh
ní fhaca said

ní fhacthas*

FUTURE

feicfidh mé
feicfidh tú
feicfidh sé
feicfidh sí
feicimid
feicfidh sibh
feicfidh siad

feicfear*

CONDITIONAL

d'fheicfinn
d'fheicfeá
d'fheicfeadh sé
d'fheicfeadh sí
d'fheicfimis
d'fheicfeadh sibh
d'fheicfidís

d'fheicfí*

VERBAL NOUN

feiceáil

VERBAL ADJECTIVE

feicthe

* autonomous form

Irregular Verb Tables

7 ith (to eat)

PRESENT

ithim
itheann tú
itheann sé
itheann sí
ithimid
itheann sibh
itheann siad

itear*

PAST

d'ith mé
d'ith tú
d'ith sé
d'ith siad
d'itheamar
d'ith sibh
d'ith siad

itheadh*

FUTURE

íosfaidh mé
íosfaidh tú
íosfaidh sé
íosfaidh sí
íosfaimid
íosfaidh sibh
íosfaidh siad

íosfar*

VERBAL NOUN

ithe

PRESENT SUBJUNCTIVE

ithe mé
ithe tú
ithe sé
ithe sí
ithimid
ithe sibh
ithe siad

itear*

IMPERATIVE

ithim
ith
itheadh sé
itheadh sí
ithimis
ithigí
ithidís

itear*

CONDITIONAL

d'íosfainn
d'íosfá
d'íosfadh sé
d'íosfadh sí
d'íosfaimis
d'íosfadh sibh
d'íosfaidís

d'íosfaí*

VERBAL ADJECTIVE

ite

8 **tabhair** (to give, take)

PRESENT

tugaim
tugann tú
tugann sé
tugann sí
tugaimid
tugann sibh
tugann said

tugtar*

PRESENT SUBJUNCTIVE

tuga mé
tuga tú
tuga sé
tuga sí
tugaimid
tuga sibh
tuga siad

tugtar*

PAST

thug mé
thug tú
thug sé
thug sí
thugamar
thug sibh
thug said

tugadh*

IMPERATIVE

tugaim
tabhair
tugadh sé
tugadh sí
tugaimis
tugaigí
tugaidís

tugtar*

FUTURE

tabharfaidh mé
tabharfaidh tú
tabharfaidh sé
tabharfaidh sí
tabharfaimid
tabharfaidh sibh
tabharfaidh said

tabharfar*

CONDITIONAL

thabharfainn
thabharfá
thabharfadh sé
thabharfadh sí
thabharfaimis
thabharfadh sibh
thabharfaidís

thabharfaí*

VERBAL NOUN

tabhairt

VERBAL ADJECTIVE

tugtha

* autonomous form

9 tar (to come, arrive, *etc*)

PRESENT	PRESENT SUBJUNCTIVE
tagaim	taga mé
tagann tú	taga tú
tagann sé	taga sé
tagann sí	taga sí
tagaimid	tagaimid
tagann sibh	taga sibh
tagann said	taga siad
tagtar*	tagtar*

PAST	IMPERATIVE
tháinig mé	tagaim
tháinig tú	tar
tháinig sé	tagadh sé
tháinig sí	tagadh sí
thángamar	tagaimis
tháinig sibh	tagaigí
tháinig said	tagaidís
thángthas*	tagtar*

FUTURE	CONDITIONAL
tiocfaidh mé	thiocfainn
tiocfaidh tú	thiocfá
tiocfaidh sé	thiocfadh sé
tiocfaidh sí	thiocfadh sí
tiocfaimid	thiocfaimis
tiocfaidh sibh	thiocfadh sibh
tiocfaidh said	thiocfaidís
tiocfar*	thiocfaí*

VERBAL NOUN	VERBAL ADJECTIVE
teacht	tagtha

10 **téigh** (to go)

PRESENT

téim
téann tú
téann sé
téann sí
téimid
téann sibh
téann said

téitear*

PRESENT SUBJUNCTIVE

té mé
té tú
té sé
té sí
téimid
té sibh
té siad

téitear*

PAST (INDEPENDENT)

chuaigh mé
chuaigh tú
chuaigh sé
chuaigh sí
chuamar
chuaigh sibh
chuaigh said

chuathas*

IMPERATIVE

téim
téigh
téadh sé
téadh sí
téimis
téigí
téidís

téitear*

PAST (DEPENDENT)

ní dheachaigh mé	ní dheachamar
go ndeachaigh mé	go ndeachamar
ní dheachaigh tú	ní dheachaigh sibh
go ndeachaigh tú	go ndeachaigh sibh
ní dheachaigh sé	ní dheachaigh said
go ndeachaigh sé	go ndeachaigh siad
ní dheachaigh sí	
go ndeachaigh sí	

ní dheachthas*

FUTURE

rachaidh mé
rachaidh tú
rachaidh sé
rachaidh sí
rachaimid
rachaidh sibh
rachaidh siad

rachfar*

CONDITIONAL

rachainn
rachfá
rachadh sé
rachadh sí
rachaimis
rachadh sibh
rachaidís

rachfaí*

VERBAL NOUN

dul

VERBAL ADJECTIVE

dulta

* autonomous form

11 **cluin/clois** (to hear)

(irregular in past only)

PAST

chuala mé
chuala tú
chuala sé
chuala sí
chualamar
chuala sibh
chuala siad
chualathas*

VERBAL NOUN OF CLUIN

cluinstin

VERBAL NOUN OF CLOIS

cloisteáil

VERBAL ADJECTIVE OF CLUIN

cluinte

VERBAL ADJECTIVE OF CLOIS

cloiste

---

12 **bailigh** (to collect, gather, *etc*)

PRESENT	PRESENT SUBJUNCTIVE
bailím	bailí mé
bailíonn tú	bailí tú
bailíonn sé	bailí sé
bailíonn sí	bailí sí
bailímid	bailímid
bailíonn sibh	bailí sibh
bailíonn said	bailí siad
bailítear*	bailítear*

PAST	IMPERATIVE
bhailigh mé	bailím
bhailigh tú	bailigh
bhailigh sé	bailíodh sé
bhailigh sí	bailíodh sí
bhailíomar	bailímis
bhailigh sibh	bailígí
bhailigh said	bailídís
bailíodh*	bailítear*

FUTURE	CONDITIONAL
baileoidh mé	bhaileoinn
baileoidh tú	bhaileofá
baileoidh sé	bhaileodh sé
baileoidh sí	bhaileodh sí
baileoimid	bhaileoimis
baileoidh sibh	bhaileodh sibh
baileoidh said	bhaileoidís
baileofar*	bhaileofaí*

VERBAL NOUN	VERBAL ADJECTIVE
bailiú	bailithe

* autonomous form

13 **beannaigh** (to bless)

PRESENT

beannaím
beannaigh
beannaíodh sé
beannaíodh sí
beannaímis
beannaígí
beannaídís

beannaítear*

PRESENT SUBJUNCTIVE

beannaí mé
beannaí tú
beannaí sé
beannaí sí
beannaímid
beannaí sibh
beannaí siad

beannaítear*

PAST

bheannaigh mé
bheannaigh tú
bheannaigh sé
bheannaigh sí
bheannaíomar
bheannaigh sibh
bheannaigh said

beannaíodh*

IMPERATIVE

beannaím
beannaigh
beannaíodh sé
beannaíodh sí
beannaímis
beannaígí
beannaídís

beannaítear*

FUTURE

beannóidh mé
beannóidh tú
beannóidh sé
beannóidh sí
beannóimid
beannóidh sibh
beannóidh said

beannófar*

CONDITIONAL

bheannóinn
bheannófá
bheannódh sé
bheannódh sí
bheannóimis
bheannódh sibh
bheannóidís

bheannófaí*

VERBAL NOUN

beannú

VERBAL ADJECTIVE

beannaithe

14 **béic** (to yell)

PRESENT

béicim
béiceann tú
béiceann sé
béiceann sí
béicimid
béiceann sibh
béiceann said

béictear*

PRESENT SUBJUNCTIVE

béice mé
béice tú
béice sé
béice sí
béicimid
béice sibh
béice said

béictear*

PAST

bhéic mé
bhéic tú
bhéic sé
bhéic sí
bhéiceamar
bhéic sibh
bhéic said

béiceadh*

IMPERATIVE

béicim
béic
béiceadh sé
béiceadh sí
béicimis
béicigí
béicidís

béictear*

FUTURE

beicfidh mé
béicfidh tú
béicfidh sé
béicfidh sí
béicfimid
béicfidh sibh
béicfidh said

béicfear*

CONDITIONAL

bhéicfinn
bhéicfeá
bhéicfeadh sé
bhéicfeadh sí
bhéicfimis
bhéicfeadh sibh
bheicfidís

bhéicfí*

VERBAL NOUN

béicí

VERBAL ADJECTIVE

béicthe

* autonomous form

15 **bog** (to move)

PRESENT

bogaim
bogann tú
bogann sé
bogann sí
bogaimid
bogann sibh
bogann said

bogtar*

PRESENT SUBJUNCTIVE

boga mé
boga tú
boga sé
boga sí
bogaimid
boga sibh
boga siad

bogtar*

PAST

bhog mé
bhog tú
bhog sé
bhog sí
bhogamar
bhog sibh
bhog said

bogadh*

IMPERATIVE

bogaim
bog
bogadh sé
bogadh sí
bogaimis
bogaigí
bogaidís

bogtar*

FUTURE

bogfaidh mé
bogfaidh tú
bogfaidh sé
bogfaidh sí
bogfaimid
bogfaidh sibh
bogfaidh said

bogfar*

CONDITIONAL

bhogfainn
bhogfá
bhogfadh sé
bhogfadh sí
bhogfaimis
bhogfadh sibh
bhogfaidís

bhogfaí*

VERBAL NOUN

bogadh

VERBAL ADJECTIVE

bogtha

16 **bris** (to break)

PRESENT

brisim
briseann tú
briseann sé
briseann sí
brisimid
briseann sibh
briseann said

bristear*

PRESENT SUBJUNCTIVE

brise mé
brise tú
brise sé
brise sí
brisimid
brise sibh
brise siad

bristear*

PAST

bhris mé
bhris tú
bhris sé
bhris sí
bhriseamar
bhris sibh
bhris said

briseadh*

IMPERATIVE

brisim
bris
briseadh sé
briseadh sí
brisimis
brisigí
brisidís

bristear*

FUTURE

brisfidh mé
bhris tú
bhris sé
bhris sí
bhriseamar
bhris sibh
bhris said

brisfear*

CONDITIONAL

bhrisfinn
bhrisfeá
bhrisfeadh sé
bhrisfeadh sí
bhrisfimis
bhrisfeadh sibh
bhrisfidís

bhrisfí*

VERBAL NOUN

briseadh

VERBAL ADJECTIVE

briste

* autonomous form

17 **caith** (to throw, wear, *etc*)

PRESENT

caithim
caitheann tú
caitheadh sé
caitheadh sí
caithimis
caithigí
caithidís

caitear*

PAST

chaith mé
chaith tú
chaith sé
chaith sí
chaitheamar
chaith sibh
chaith said

caitheadh*

FUTURE

caithfidh mé
caithfidh tú
caithfidh sé
caithfidh sí
caithfimid
caithfidh sibh
caithfidh said

caithfear*

VERBAL NOUN

caitheamh

PRESENT SUBJUNCTIVE

caithe mé
caithe tú
caithe sé
caithe sí
caithimid
caithe sibh
caithe siad

caitear*

IMPERATIVE

caithim
caitheann tú
caitheann sé
caitheann sí
caithimid
caitheann sibh
caitheann said

caitear*

CONDITIONAL

chaithfinn
chaithfeá
chaithfeadh sé
chaithfeadh sí
chaithfimis
chaithfeadh sibh
chaithfidís

chaithfí*

VERBAL ADJECTIVE

caite

18 ceiliúir (to celebrate)

PRESENT

ceiliúraim
ceiliúrann tú
ceiliúrann sé
ceiliúrann sí
ceiliúraimid
ceiliúrann sibh
ceiliúrann said

ceiliúrtar*

PRESENT SUBJUNCTIVE

ceiliúra mé
ceiliúra tú
ceiliúra sé
ceiliúra sí
ceiliúraimid
ceiliúra sibh
ceiliúra siad

ceiliúrtar*

PAST

cheiliúir mé
cheiliúir tú
cheiliúir sé
cheiliúir sí
cheiliúramar
cheiliúir sibh
cheiliúir said

ceiliúradh*

IMPERATIVE

ceiliúraim
ceiliúir
ceiliúradh sé
ceiliúradh sí
ceiliúraimis
ceiliúraigí
ceiliúraidís

ceiliúrtar*

FUTURE

ceiliúrfaidh mé
ceiliúrfaidh tú
ceiliúrfaidh sé
ceiliúrfaidh sí
ceiliúrfaimid
ceiliúrfaidh sibh
ceiliúrfaidh said

ceiliúrfar*

CONDITIONAL

cheiliúrfainn
cheiliúrfá
cheiliúrfadh sé
cheiliúrfadh sí
cheiliúrfaimis
cheiliúrfadh sibh
cheiliúrfaidis

cheiliúrfaí*

VERBAL NOUN

ceiliúradh

VERBAL ADJECTIVE

ceiliúrtha

* autonomous form

19 **cloígh** (to defeat)

PRESENT

cloím
cloíonn tú
cloíonn sé
cloíonn sí
cloímid
cloíonn sibh
cloíonn said

cloítear*

PRESENT SUBJUNCTIVE

cloí mé
cloí tú
cloí sé
cloí sí
cloímid
cloí sibh
cloí siad

cloítear*

PAST

chloígh mé
chloígh tú
chloígh sé
chloígh sí
chloíomar
chloígh sibh
chloígh said

cloíodh*

IMPERATIVE

cloím
cloígh
cloíodh sé
cloíodh sí
cloímis
cloíonn sibh
cloíonn said

cloítear*

FUTURE

cloífidh mé
cloífidh tú
cloífidh sé
cloífidh sí
cloífimid
cloífidh sibh
cloífidh said

cloífear*

CONDITIONAL

chloífinn
chloífeá
chloífeadh sé
chloífeadh sí
chloífimis
chloífeadh sibh
chloífidís

chloífí*

VERBAL NOUN

cloí

VERBAL ADJECTIVE

cloíte

20 cosain (to defend, cost)

PRESENT
cosnaím
cosnaíonn tú
cosnaíonn sé
cosnaíonn sí
cosnaímid
cosnaíonn sibh
cosnaíonn said

cosnaítear*

PRESENT SUBJUNCTIVE
cosnaí mé
cosnaí tú
cosnaí sé
cosnaí sí
cosnaímid
cosnaí sibh
cosnaí siad

cosnaítear*

PAST
chosain mé
chosain tú
chosain sé
chosain sí
chosnaíomar
chosain sibh
chosain said

cosnaíodh*

IMPERATIVE
cosnaím
cosain
cosnaíodh sé
cosnaíodh sí
cosnaímis
cosnaígí
cosnaídís

cosnaítear*

FUTURE
cosnóidh mé
cosnóidh tú
cosnóidh sé
cosnóidh sí
cosnóimid
cosnóidh sibh
cosnóidh said

cosnófar*

CONDITIONAL
chosnóinn
chosnófá
chosnódh sé
chosnódh sí
chosnóimis
chosnódh sibh
chosnóidís

chosnófaí*

VERBAL NOUN
cosaint

VERBAL ADJECTIVE
cosanta

* autonomous form

21 **feoigh** (to wither)

PRESENT

feoim
feonn tú
feonn sé
feonn sí
feoimid
feonn sibh
feonn said

feoitear*

PRESENT SUBJUNCTIVE

feo mé
feo tú
feo sé
feo sí
feoimid
feo sibh
feo said

feoitear*

PAST

d'fheoigh mé
d'fheoigh tú
d'fheoigh sé
d'fheoigh sí
d'fheomar
feofaidh sibh
feofaidh said

feodh*

IMPERATIVE

feoim
feoigh
feodh sé
feodh sí
feoimis
feoigí
feoidís

feoitear*

FUTURE

feofaidh mé
feofaidh tú
feofaidh sé
feofaidh sí
feofaimid
feofaidh sibh
feofaidh said

feofar*

CONDITIONAL

d'fheofainn
d'fheofá
d'fheofadh sé
d'fheofadh sí
d'fheofaimis
d'fheofadh sibh
d'fheofaidís

d'fheofaí*

VERBAL NOUN

feo

VERBAL ADJECTIVE

feoite

22 imir (to play)

PRESENT

imrím
imríonn tú
imríonn sé
imríonn sí
imrímid
imríonn sibh
imríonn said

imrítear*

PAST

d'imir mé
d'imir tú
d'imir sé
d'imir sí
d'imríomar
d'imir sibh
d'imir said

imríodh*

FUTURE

imreoidh mé
imreoidh tú
imreoidh sé
imreoidh sí
imreoimid
imreoidh sibh
imreoidh said

imreofar*

VERBAL NOUN

imirt

PRESENT SUBJUNCTIVE

imrí mé
imrí tú
imrí sé
imrí sí
imrímid
imrí sibh
imrí siad

imrítear*

IMPERATIVE

imrím
imir
imríodh sé
imríodh sí
imrímis
imrígí
imrídís

imrítear*

CONDITIONAL

d'imreoinn
d'imreofá
d'imreodh sé
d'imreodh sí
d'imreoimis
d'imreodh sibh
d'imreoidís

d'imreofaí*

VERBAL ADJECTIVE

imeartha

* autonomous form

23 **luigh** (to lie, set)

PRESENT

luím
luíonn tú
luíonn sé
luíonn sí
luímid
luíonn sibh
luíonn said

luitear*

PRESENT SUBJUNCTIVE

luí mé
luí tú
luí sé
luí sí
luímid
luí sibh
luí siad

luitear*

PAST

luigh mé
luigh tú
luigh sé
luigh sí
luíomar
luigh sibh
luigh said

luíodh*

IMPERATIVE

luím
luigh
luíodh sé
luíodh sé
luímis
luígí
luídís

luitear*

FUTURE

luífidh mé
luífidh tú
luífidh sé
luífidh sí
luífimid
luífidh sibh
luífidh said

luífear*

CONDITIONAL

luífinn
luífeá
luífeadh sé
luífeadh sí
luífimis
luífeadh sibh
luífidís

luífí*

VERBAL NOUN

luí

VERBAL ADJECTIVE

luite

24   **mol** (to praise, advise)

PRESENT
molaim
molann tú
molann sé
molann sí
molaimid
molann sibh
molann said
moltar*

PRESENT SUBJUNCTIVE
mola mé
mola tú
mola sé
mola sí
molaimid
mola sibh
mola siad
moltar*

PAST
mhol mé
mhol tú
mhol sé
mhol sí
mholamar
mhol sibh
mhol said
moladh*

IMPERATIVE
molaim
mol
moladh sé
moladh sí
molaimis
molaigí
molaidís
moltar*

FUTURE
molfaidh mé
molfaidh tú
molfaidh sé
molfaidh sí
molfaimid
molfaidh sibh
molfaidh said
molfar*

CONDITIONAL
mholfainn
mholfá
mholfadh sé
mholfadh sí
mholfaimis
mholfadh sibh
mholfaidís
mholfaí*

VERBAL NOUN
moladh

VERBAL ADJECTIVE
molta

* autonomous form

25 **sáigh** (to stab)

PRESENT

sáim
sánn tú
sánn sé
sánn sí
sáimid
sánn sibh
sánn said

sáitear*

PRESENT SUBJUNCTIVE

sá mé
sá tú
sá sé
sá sí
sáimid
sá sibh
sá siad

sáitear*

PAST

sháigh mé
sháigh tú
sháigh sé
sháigh sí
shámar
sháigh sibh
sháigh said

sádh*

IMPERATIVE

sáim
sáigh
sádh sé
sádh sí
sáimis
sáigí
sáidís

sáitear*

FUTURE

sáfaidh mé
sáfaidh tú
sáfaidh sé
sáfaidh sí
sáfaimid
sáfaidh sibh
sáfaidh said

sáfar*

CONDITIONAL

sháfainn
sháfá
sháfadh sé
sháfadh sí
sháfaimis
sháfadh sibh
sháfaidís

sháfaí*

VERBAL NOUN

sá

VERBAL ADJECTIVE

sáite

26 **sóinseáil** (to change)

PRESENT

sóinseálaim
sóinseálann tú
sóinseálann sé
sóinseálann sí
sóinseálaimid
sóinseálann sibh
sóinseálann said

sóinseáiltear*

PRESENT SUBJUNCTIVE

sóinseála mé
sóinseála tú
sóinseála sé
sóinseála sí
sóinseálaimid
sóinseála sibh
sóinseála siad

sóinseáiltear*

PAST

shóinseáil mé
shóinseáil tú
shóinseáil sé
shóinseáil sí
shóinseálamar
shóinseáil sibh
shóinseáil said

sóinseáladh*

IMPERATIVE

sóinseálaim
sóinseáil
sóinseáladh sé
sóinseáladh sí
sóinseálaimis
sóinseálaigí
sóinseáilidís

sóinseáiltear**

FUTURE

sóinseálfaidh mé
sóinseálfaidh tú
sóinseálfaidh sé
sóinseálfaidh sí
sóinseálfaimid
sóinseálfaidh sibh
sóinseálfaidh said

sóinseálfar*

CONDITIONAL

shóinseálfainn
shóinseálfá
shóinseálfadh sé
shóinseálfadh sí
shóinseálfaimis
shóinseálfadh sibh
shóinseálfaidís

shóinseálfaí*

VERBAL NOUN

sóinseáil

VERBAL ADJECTIVE

sóinseáilte

VERB INDEX

HOW TO USE THE VERB INDEX

The verbs in bold are the model verbs which you will find in the verb tables. All the other verbs follow one of these patterns, so the number next to each verb indicates which pattern fits this particular verb. For example, **ceap** (*to think*) follows the same pattern as **bog** (number 15 in the verb tables).

All the verbs are in alphabetical order. Some verbs are followed by their verbal noun and verbal adjective if they differ from their verb model. This is indicated by *vb n* and *vb adj* respectively.

abair	1	beathaigh	13
admhaigh (*vb n* admháil)	13	**béic**	14
aimsigh	11	**beir**	2
aistrigh	11	beirigh	11
aithin	22	**bí**	3
aithris (*3rd pres* aithrisíonn, *vb n* aithris)	20	bisigh	11
		blais	16
alp (*vb adj* alptha)	24	blaistigh	11
altaigh	13	bocáil	26
amharc (*vb adj* amhartha, *vb n* amharc)	24	bodhraigh	13
		bog	15
aontaigh	13	bolaigh	13
ardaigh	13	braith	17
athchúrsáil	26	breathnaigh	13
athraigh	13	**bris**	16
babhtáil	26	brostaigh	13
bac	15	brúcht (*vb adj* brúchta)	26
bácáil	26	brúigh	25
bagair (*vb adj* bagartha)	20	bruith (*vb n* bruith)	17
báigh	25	buaigh (*vb n* buachan)	25
bailigh	12	buail (*vb n* bualadh)	16
bain (*vb n* baint)	16	buair (*vb n* buaireamh, *vb adj* buartha)	12
bánaigh	13		
básaigh	13	buamáil	26
basc (*vb adj* basctha)	24	búir (*vb n* búireach)	12
beannaigh	13	bunaigh	13
bearr	15	cabhraigh	13
beartaigh	13	cáiligh	11

More fantastic titles in the Collins Irish Dictionary range:

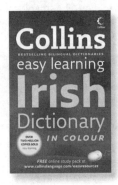

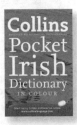